VITAL
VOGUE

People want to be loved; failing that admired; failing that feared; failing that hated and despised. They want to evoke some sort of sentiment. The soul shudders before oblivion and seeks connection at any price.

Hjalmar Soderberg

Photos by Ari and Zoe Elefterin

Illustrations in the style of Reich, mixed with Maturana & Varela

Author: Otto von Busch

ISBN: 978-91-984047-1-5
New York: SelfPassage 2018

Second edition (October 2018) after exhibition at Aronson Gallery, The New School, NYC
Errors and omissions will be corrected in subsequent editions.

VITAL VOGUE

A BIOSOCIAL PERSPECTIVE ON FASHION

OTTO VON BUSCH

In 1940 the psychoanalyst, political theorist, biologist and pioneer of body therapies Wilhelm Reich taught at The New School. His course, "Character Formation: Biological and Sociological Aspects," introduced students to the outlines of Reich's theories of psychosomatic dynamics, and how the psyche is caught between the bioelectrical energies of the body and social currents, between arousal and anxiety, freedom and fascism. How would a fashion student attending Reich's class have interpreted his ideas and put to use in the realm of dress? This is the point of departure for the exhibition *Vital Vogue* at Parsons School of Design in March/April 2018 from which this book is a part.

While the task of the project has been to interpret Reich's ideas into the realm of fashion and connect theories that correspond with Reich's perspective, the challenge has been to avoid some of the recklessness which comes easily in artistic appropriation. The intention has been to highlight not only the relevance of Reich to the study of fashion, but also how his ideas are uniquely situated at the intersection between affect, new materialism, embodiment and political theory. Reich's biosocial approach today rings curiously contemporary and his work binds these theoretical fields together into a daring and visionary whole. Vital Vogue is a designerly *provotype* emerging from Reich's work, with the aim of provoking new ideas of what fashion can be.[1]

It is however unavoidable that a project like this distorts the original teachings. As a student of Reich, I have missed a whole lot, misread other parts and finally dragged his ideas into a whole different field. All the mistakes are entirely mine and I recommend readers to go to the undiluted sources of Reich's own texts.

This second edition of *Vital Vogue*, from October 2018, contains some minor edits of text and endnotes. At the end of this volume, the reader can find documentation from the project exhibition at the Aronson Gallery as well as questionnaires for exploring the energetic charge of fashion.

CONTENTS

*Getting turned on is a process that engages the whole self.
Our arousal is an endorsement of a range of surprisingly
articulate suggestions as to how we might live.*

Alain de Botton (2012: 46)

FASHION IS FLIRTING

In an everyday sense of the word, fashion suggests two common connotations. Firstly, we think fashion is about clothes, goods, accessories and brands, and that these commodities are symbolic markers of identity. Secondly, that fashion is shallow and thus an illusion, where the propaganda of the industry hypnotizes and fools people, even those who use it to their advantage. Fashion is thus a bit like Christmas; some refuse to take part, while others play along because they like the mood, lights, rituals and gifts, yet none of us really believe in Santa.[2] From such perspective, fashion is deemed a conspiracy of sorts, carried out by advertisers or media, profiting on our vanity while trapping poor narcissists into debt. The sweet language of style and taste seduces people, yet their interest in fashion makes them somewhat deceived, or perhaps worse: willing *collaborateurs* with an evil and unsustainable industry. Yet, if we place fashion primarily into commodities and illusions, it can be hard to understand the deep desires of fashion; how fashion is anchored in emotions, affects and embodied desires of its users.[3] What if people are not fooled by fashion as an "opium" of irrationality, but truly *desire* fashion, what it does to their bodies, even when its ideals work against them and they become its victims?

We could start to explore fashion from the agency and sensations of the body. When fashion works at its best, we *feel it in our bodies*. It may be a sense of excitement, allure, or arousal. Fashion is a passion, a sensibility of aesthetic desire, an ephemeral wave of pleasurable anticipation rushing through the body. It is sexually charged, but not necessarily in a narrow, genital sense. Fashion can trigger our erotic imagination, a stirring dream world, but as with sexual fantasies, this may include a wide variety of relationships, events and scenarios that are not always explicit nor speak to our more rational side. When fashion works on us, it changes our posture. We feel seen and on top of things. We expand emotionally, socially, and bodily, opening up our sensibilities towards the world. We feel a plasmatic pulse of energy streaming along the spine and through our limbs. The eye contact, the affirmative comments and looks; it's like a kick, and once you have experienced it you cannot get enough. Yes, at its best, fashion is that thrill of appreciation and adoration and a surge of aliveness sweeping like a wave of pleasure through the body.

But when fashion *does not work*, we also feel it in our bodies. We feel the anxiety, humiliation, and shame that emanates from what is jokingly called a "wardrobe malfunction." We may not pay attention to it in an everyday occasion or when we have no witnesses around, but like a numb limb or broken tool, we first recognize it in the moment of failure, we realize the agonizing effects of the enclothed wound. The anxiety makes us cringe, our posture changes, we feel wounded, contract into a ball and try to escape from sight like a suffering animal. We may rationally know that looks do not matter, but the experience of social pain in a humiliating situation may be just too much to bear. Fashion connects not merely to our identity, but to the emotional grounding of the body, the very core of our biological being.

We are born free, and in most societies we can dress however we want, yet why do so few of us play with the way we dress in more daring ways? Are there emotions that hold us back? As children we love to dress up and play a wide variety of characters. We are princesses and cowboys, unicorns and dinosaurs, superheroes and doctors, agents and thieves. We use dress to accentuate our dream worlds and playfully enact a rich variety of selves. However, at school we soon come to see that clothes and dress manners are important social regulators. We come to sort not only our peers but also our own emotions around dress; what is considered masculine and feminine, cool or uncool, etc. Even if we are taught that dress is only shallow, and we should not judge people by what they wear, we often come to mediate our social relationships through dress, and also our own moods. We experience how clothes signify and communicate, and in the process of forming a wardrobe and identity that is acceptable and successful, we forget the playfulness, pleasures and aesthetic imagination of clothing. We are born free, but everywhere held in chain-stores. Somehow, we come to desire our velvet chains of safe conformity.

Whereas some garments come to feel like a safe haven from unwanted attention and comments, other garments help us take risks, engage and move socially and emotionally. They help us reach out and touch our social surrounding. On such occasions we may feel alive as people respond to our appearance and we can feel the touch of their perception, their looks. However, the same looks may feel uncomfortable when it happens in the wrong setting or from an unwanted source. In some occasions it may even be an attention tainted by fear.

These tensions around the biosocial emotions of fashion make many feel unease around the play of attention and imagination with clothes. We may escape into a safe uniform of jeans and t-shirts, even if these may still have the cuts, colors and marks of hierarchies. Each community has a normative baseline of dress that avoids risk; the local team colors. But taking any risk puts the user at the mercy of his or her peers, being called upon one's dress to be "boyish" or "girlish" or garments being too "preppy" or "slutty" or "emo" or "jocky" etc. The judgments of dress define our emotional as well as social stature.

Thus, very early, we move from a realm of dressed fantasy play and limitless imagination into a world of emotions and relations that are funneled through the commodities of dress, fashion and pre-packaged identities. Our desires get drawn into a realm of aesthetic limitations, while we crave contact and emotional connection. We begin not only to judge the character and value of others by what they wear, but also turn the verdict onto ourselves.[4] We become fearful of what people may think of us. As social groupings in school intensify in teenage years, with in-groups and out-groups, the popular clique and the excluded nerds, we start dressing with anxiety. Fashion becomes a sensitive realm where we fear "wardrobe malfunctions" and bad hair days.

Many of us forget the pleasure and playfulness of dress and connect the act of taking risks with a sense of danger and anxiety. We seek acceptable habits of identity and very few come to experience the full transformational qualities of dress. The occasions of dressing up for identity play get restricted to masquerades and clubs where people can experience their own sense of "coming out," which to many is a world beyond their imagination as they are held back by social conventions and habits. Instead, we seek leaders who will help us; designers, oracles and editors, who guide and decide for us. We become fearful of our own desires and instead seek to hide under the safety of uniforms or the cheap acceptable thrills of fast fashion. As sung in the popular TV series *Flight of the Concords;* "You think you know fashion, well fashion's a stranger, You think fashion's your friend, my friend, Fashion is danger."

As sociologist Georg Simmel posits, our everyday relationship to fashion is trapped in a paradox between uniformity and individuality, or safety and freedom, and challenging conventions can easily turn into social danger. Yet, if we look around, and perhaps also look into our own wardrobe, the balance at play most often seems titled towards the safe or conforming end of the scale. Even if most of us proudly claim we have a style of our own, we end up dressing all too much like our peers, as this seems to "feel right." In what ways can we unpack the emotional grounding of fashion in our bodies, our rationalizations, and our own urge towards conformity, even when thinking we are rebels?

In order to unpack these clashing desires of fashion we could approach it from a biosocial perspective, where the emotions of the body are tightly coupled to the affective dynamics of the social realm. The biosocial perspective on fashion in this essay primarily emerges from the works of psychoanalyst, political theorist, biologist and natural scientist Wilhelm Reich (1897–1957). Reich's ideas offer a twofold approach to fashion that helps capture two central dynamics in the emotional experience of everyday fashion. On the one hand, it helps see how *the emotions of fashion are moving the body as a biosocial energy,* how we *feel fashion* as an allure and pleasure (or promise of pleasure). On the other hand, because of its anchoring in the body, we may also *become anxious of the emotions evoked by fashion,* to fear the judgments and responses of others, which in turn draw us towards authorities. Even if Reich's original ideas do not touch on fashion specifically, his analytical framework combines embodiment and psychology with sociological and political theory, thus coupling politics and emotions. In order to enrich Reich's perspective, also other theorists will become relevant as fashion is unpacked as a biosocial phenomenon, straddled between the embodied sensations of pleasure and pain, arousal and anxiety, allure and predation.

Reich starts out as a physician and psychoanalyst, and was considered one of Sigmund Freud's most talented but controversial students. Reich is immediately captured by Freud's ideas of the libido, as a "motor force of sexual life," an "electrical field," a "quantitative energy" and "something which is capable of increase, decrease, displacement and discharge, and which extends itself over the memory traces of an idea like an electric charge over the surface of the body." (1938: 577) Yet Reich draws his own conclusions around this sexual energy of the body to open new vistas of thought and practice in the biosocial realm.[5] Firmly grounding his theory in biology and in a process he called "energetic functionalism," Reich explores whether the libido is no metaphor but in fact a material form of bioelectrical current, streaming through the body. This focus on the biology of the body makes Reich one of the early innovators of psychosomatic therapy, connecting the body to its social environment, in its cultural, sexual and socio-economic context and conditions, thus merging the biosocial realm with political theory.

Reich develops the idea of the streaming of the libido to describe a biosocial "sexual economy," or "energy household" of the organism. Energy flows through the body or is regulated by contracted muscles or inhibitions. Reich comes to call this bioelectrical energy *orgone*, primarily because he sees this energy capable of charging organic, non-conducting (insulating) substances (Reich 1970: 340f).[6] Similarly, it is specifically the movement and direction of energy, its streaming and pulsating tendencies, that makes Reich see these flows as the fundamental drivers of emotion and health.

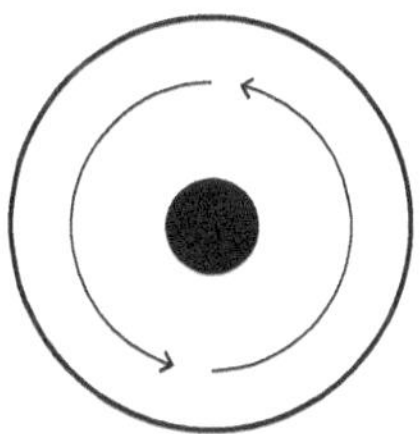

*Orgonotic system with inner sex-economic flow, centered
arond core and surrounded by periphery/membrane.*

In a healthy person's body, the energy flows and pulsates freely. But some people are "armored," with inadequate circulation of energy. The flow of emotion is held back. This armoring results in muscles binding the energy, making it stagnate. The binding corresponds between body and mind; a rigid body ties to a strict character.[7] Not only is such character prone to neurotic disorders but also to a fear of spontaneity, life and freedom.[8] Under a regime of authoritarian family and repressive social institutions, this fear of one's own life energy makes people irrational and draws them to authorities and leaders. Armored people are uncomfortable with the streaming sensations of the energy throughout their bodies, as it evokes a loss of control. Similarly, they also feel uncomfortable together with more spontaneous and free-minded spirits who are looked upon as a threatening other, someone who threatens the order of things. It is this fear of what others may think that is the foundation of the dilemma that, *"man is born free, yet he goes thought life a slave."* (Reich 1973: 467)[9] The judgment of others and avoidance of emotional self-knowledge keeps people fearful of the emotions streaming through their animal bodies.[10] Trapped in their bodies while living in their heads, fear of life and spontaneity ensnares them to their habits. The only way to mitigate the trap of this emotional armoring is to challenge the everyday repressive anxieties of people and find therapy that unlocks the muscular binding of the plasmatic energy of the body.

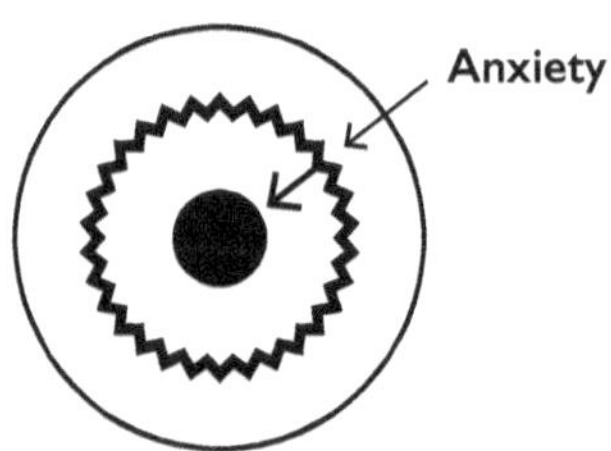

Armored orgonotic system, with muscular tensions inhibiting healthy streaming of energy, binding anxiety within

From a Reichian perspective, the human animal shares its basic functional characteristics with very simple organisms. Even if humans live and experience much of their life through the lens of culture, the basis of our being is highly organic and animalistic. Thus, as organic beings, we share the same biological functions as our primitive relatives. We are basically jellyfish, pulsating with organic life, from the single cell and all the way up to the complexity of our whole bodies. Rhythms of plasmatic excitation resonate throughout our bodies, from the heartbeat and pumping of blood, to breathing and digestion, sleep, metabolic and menstruation cycles all the way to the cycle of a lifetime itself. The organic life of the protoplasm is the "morphological forerunner" and is echoed in the function of the human autonomic nervous system (Reich 1982: 56).[11] The autonomic nervous system *"merely carries on, in an organized manner, a function which already exists in principle in animals without nervous systems; i.e., the function of* plasma movement, hydration and dehydration, contraction and expansion, tension and relaxation" (Reich 1982: 58). At the basis of these plasmatic movement in the protoplasm Reich traces the foundations of emotion. As Reich points out, "literally defined, the word 'emotion' means 'moving outwards' or 'pushing out.'" (Reich 1973: 137) He continues,

> *Fundamentally, emotion is nothing but a plasmatic movement.* Pleasurable stimuli effect an 'emotion' of the protoplasm from the center toward the periphery. Non-pleasurable stimuli, on the other hand, bring about an 'emotion' or, more correctly, 're-motion' of the protoplasm from the periphery toward the center of the organism. These two basic directions of the biophysical plasma current correspond to the two basic affects of the psychic apparatus, pleasure and anxiety." (Reich 1973: 137f)

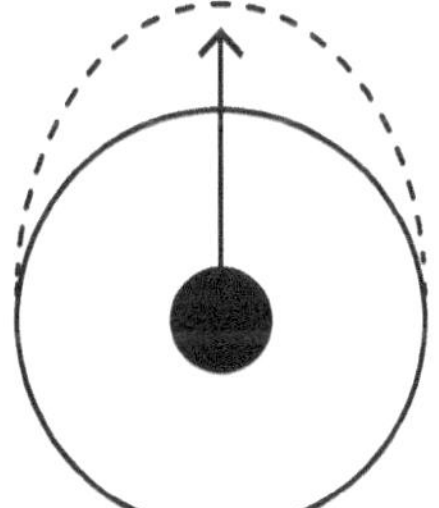
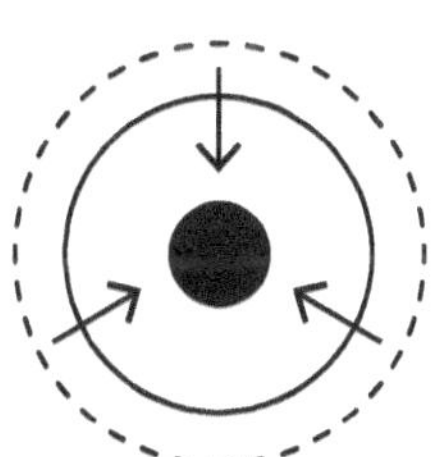

Basic functional movements of emotion (expansion/pleasure) and remotion (contraction/anxiety) in unarmored system

When curious, sensorial organs of the organism extend outwards from the body towards the world, while they retreat back into the body in anxiety. Simple examples can be the antennae of snails or the pseudopods of amoeba (Reich 1982: 35ff).[12] Such expansion and contraction, of emotion and remotion, reoccur throughout the whole organism, which functions much like a bladder. Like in breathing, one mode cannot exist without the other. Biologically the organism strives to keep its natural movements open and free, and a healthy emotional life is one of unhindered emotional dynamics as "biophysical plasma excitation transmits sensation, and a sensation expresses itself through plasma movement." (Reich 1973: 138) The mobilization and natural streaming of plasmatic currents of emotions are functionally identical to the mobilization of orgone energy, the life energy of the body and cosmos (1973: 138). The central issue here is that the "depth" of emotions extends deeper than the psyche or the realm of thought, into the body and into "the providence of protoplasmic functions, even going beyond the physiology of nerves and muscles." (1973: 139)[13]

Emotional sensation also echoes through the protoplasm, as in the "inner stirrings" of music (1973: 140) or the frissons of excitation, and is thus beyond words or rational communication. But an important component of this thesis is how the emotions of the body expand outwards into the world, beyond the boundaries of the organism. Emotions are plasmatic pressures in the organism. Reich points out how many languages reflect this, for example in the German word *Ausdruck* and the English equivalent "expression" (outward-pressure), as the language of the living organism; *"the living organism expresses itself in movements; we therefore speak of 'expressive movements.' Expressive movement is an inherent characteristic of the protoplasm."* (1973: 141)[14]

The plasmatic motility does not happen in isolation, but is instead coupled with other organisms. Emotional movements of organisms affect each other, their sensory membranes touch and relay plasmatic movements between each other, like waves throughout the social plasma. The protoplasmic movement, or ex-pressure, expands into the sensorium of another organism that thus transfers the wave to the next. An example can be the sensing of danger; "the panic reaction in the animal kingdom is based on an involuntary reproduction of the movement expressive of anxiety." (1973: 143) Such expressions "bring about *an imitation* in our own organism." (1973: 144) Emotional affects and imitations are thus physical expressions in the organism, not conscious thought patterns, but are anchored in the depths of the organism; *"the living organism functions autonomously, beyond the sphere of language, intellect, and volition."* (1973: 147) The main body of emotional functioning and social expressions are thus non-conscious, or "supra-personal" (1973: 149). In relation to current discussions around "mirror neurons," Reich sees material and embodied component in biosocial imitative behaviors.[15] Our emotional life is thus governed by excitation waves and *"biological energy is being transmitted in these wave movements."* (1973: 154) In a homology, political theorist Iris Young (2005: 69) emphasizes how touch is different from communication, as "touch immerses the subject in fluid continuity with the object, and for the touching subject the object touched reciprocates the touching, blurring the border between self and other."

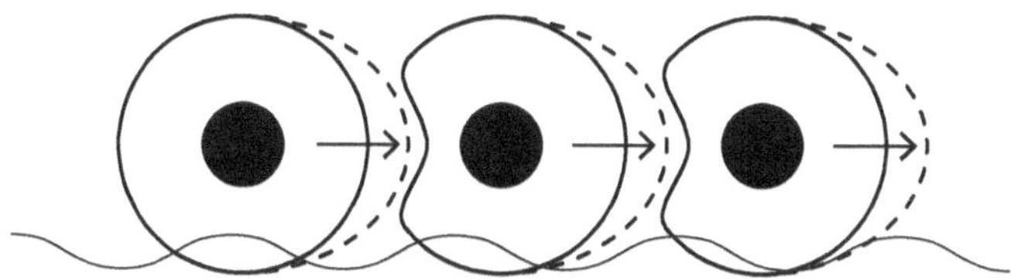

Relay of plasmatic motility, as apparent in waves
of imitation and diffusion of affects

As with the "inner stirrings" evoked by music, an analogy between fashion and music is not far fetched. Like in fashion there are trends and recurrent themes in music styles. The anticipation of new rhythms, tunes and sounds, excites people, producing an endless desire for new songs and artists. The pulsations of music also have the ability to break the isolation between individuals, doomed by their membranes to remain separated, and dancing is the recurrent playground of passion and flirting. Rhythms echo between the organic plasma of bodies, making peers move to the same beat even if separated. It is music that brings them together in an undeniable unity, deeper than what language can bring about: their bodies pulsate together while separate. It is this sense of unity that also brings about a micro-utopian state between musicians, listeners and dancers. Fashion, like music, leaves a sense of discharge, exhaustion, relaxation, if not haunting loss.[16]

The closest connection between two fluid bodies happens in the sexual act, and is, at its best, an unmediated fusion between two orgonotic systems as the sexual process *"is the biological-productive energy process per se."* (Reich 1982: 128f) From Reich's perspective, the sexual act is essentially an electrical process of excitation and charge followed by discharge and relaxation, whereby the orgasmic convulsions of the body signal healthy plasmatic motility throughout the organism.[17] "In the sexual act, two bioelectrically highly charged organisms come into contact with one another," and in their merger, "two bodies experiencing orgastic ecstasy are nothing more than a quivering mass of plasm." (Reich 1982: 13)[18] The psychosomatic function of the orgasm is to release built up tension, pleasure and a wholesome surrender to this orgasmic motility unties emotional contractions. However, armoring inhibits this motility, corrupting the sexual action with anxiety, shame, egotism and violence, a fate similar to that of the primary and playful act of flirting.[19]

A Reich-inspired perspective opens some exciting avenues of thought in relation to fashion. Firstly, we can radically rethink *fashion as energy*, and secondly, the social phenomenon of fashion is *the transmission of this energy*. Like orgone, this energy can change organic (insulating) materials such as everyday clothing, and it is essentially connecting waves of social excitation with plasmatic movements in the body, that is, *conveying fashion into passion*.[20] A new look sweeps across the social field like a wave of an energetic force, moving all affected bodies floating on the surface of enclothed sensibility, transmitting this force into plasmatic motility. It is indeed a "passion" that spreads like wild fire; neurons firing from the seductive energy of allure and arousal; new sensibilities matched with new looks; a network of bodies ready for new dopamine charges. Passion is an energy that pulsates through the body awaking the emotional sensorium. But passion is also erotic, that is, a force of imagination, a vitalisation of desire and anticipation. It is a process, defined by movement, as fashion "never is, it is always becoming." (Simmel 1957)[21] Thus fashion is a wave of anticipation, a connection, a sense of frisson. We use fashion to dream up a world of becoming, and even if not always eroticized, it builds up suspense and expectations – a becoming as a process, pointing to pleasure and the arousing ascent towards coming.

To Reich, the function of the orgasm unlocks the basis of the motility of organisms as it manifests the unity of living functioning, because as he sees it, *"the sexual process, that is, the expansive biological process of pleasure, is the productive life-process per se."* (Reich 1970: xxi)

The sexual process of motility follows a wave-like pattern, first of excitation and expansion, followed by release and contraction. What he calls the "orgasm formula" is functionally analogous; mechanical tension and bioelectrical charge are followed by bioelectrical discharge and mechanical relaxation. "The basic function of all living matter, namely tension and relaxation, charge and discharge, is represented here in its purest form." (Reich 1982: 9) This "TC-function" (tension-charge) is the life-formula itself, and can, according to Reich, be studied in all living organisms, from the primitive mollusk to the complex human body. It is the pulse of all organic movement.

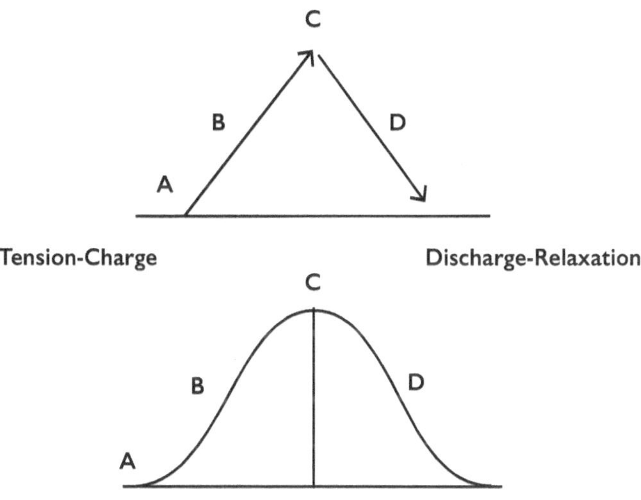

Top: Reich's model of the orgasm formula or TC-function, with,
A; forepleasure, B; excitation, C; climax, D; relaxation.

Bottom: Everett Roger's diffusion of innovation model (1962) of how ideas spread,
with, A; innovators, B; early adopters, C; majority, D; laggards.

Bioelectrical charge in the body is not merely mechanical. Imagination plays an important part in explaining human excitation as "an idea, endowed with a very small amount of energy, [is] capable of provoking an *increase* of excitation. The excitation thus provoked, in turn [makes] the idea vivid and forceful." (Reich 1970: 71) It is the capacity to *surrender* to these plasmatic energies Reich calls "orgastic potency," that is, "*the complete discharge of all dammed-up sexual excitation* through *involuntary pleasurable contractions of the body."* (Reich 1970: 79) The relationship between tension and discharge is what produces the pleasures of excitation.[22]

The nature of orgone energy is a much debated and considered by many as quasi-science, not least since court convicted Reich of fraud in 1956 in a case instigated by the Federal Drug Administration.[23] Whatever its scientific status, Reich biographer Robert Corrington (2003: xxi) argues the orgone theory has "strong metaphoric value, but it may also have some direct phenomenological warrant." As Reich pointed out, this energy can charge organic matter, so it is important not to mystify it or make it purely metaphysical, but keep its material and bioelectrical grounding. Forcing our understanding of this energy through a distinction of objective vs. subjective, or real vs. unreal, would hide as much as it reveals, particularly in its usage to understand a phenomenon such as fashion which for its lifetime has been burdened by being seen as an unimportant illusion, diverting our attention from more objective "realities." Perhaps the most important question is instead what a fashion energy makes us able to recognize and trace in its movements and directions. In *A Foray into the Worlds of Animals and Humans* (2010), biologist Jacob von Uexkull, who is recurrently cited in Reich's work, describes how the biosemiotics within higher environmental elaborations may take the form of "magical environments," where animals start playing, use illusions and "fantastic phenomena," in their behavior. Yet, as Uexkull underlines, these worlds are not mere trick of the mind, but enact the stimuli corresponding between the organism's inner and outer environments (what Uexkull called *Umwelt/Innenwelt*), mobilizing the sensorium for biological meaning-creation in the behavior of the organism (Uexkull 2010: 119ff).

Not unlike Reich's idea of a bioelectrical charge building up and streaming through the body, we can think of fashion as a life force in the sense that it translates agency and affects. A Reich-inspired perspective on fashion is in this sense homologous to a "vibrancy" of social and physical matter (Bennett 2010). If we accept that objects have agency, that they affect us, as they do in "new materialism" (Fox & Alldred 2017), we can see how they also transmit plasmatic motilities in the body, and this makes fashion a vital and alluring energy streaming through the social realm. Social arrangements are formed and stirred through emotional transmissions, much in accordance with the last decades' discussions of the "affective turn" (Clough 2010).[24] Not unlike an electrical waveform, its currents oscillate between the heights of the new and the lows of the dead duds, which are drained of charge. This notion of fashion resonates with sociologist Gabriel Tarde's notion of how the social object, or "germ," is "trapped between pure repetition, endurance and continuity on the one hand, and on the other, pure vibration, pure potential." (Lepinay 2007: 526)[25] What Tarde calls "germ capital" is much like an energy, as it cannot be accumulated as it becomes dead and worthless when it loses vibration, intensity and passion. In a similar way, a new fashion is vibrant and alive as the wave of a new trend hits consumers with a rush of excitement, with early adoption, then upwards towards the height of popularity, followed by a quick fall from grace and what was not long ago a "must have" is now recognized as dull and uninteresting. Clothes can be saved and amassed, but fashion dies quickly in captivity.[26]

Applying Reich's perspective of biosocial energy and plasmatic motility to the realm of fashion would rearrange the spatial configuration of agency and action within the everyday realm of fashion. The locus of fashion is not in the "system" or in the "industry," even if these are its commoditized vectors, that is, the channels or infrastructure through which most of the energy is fashion transmitted. Instead of being out there, in the system, an energetic perspective puts the locus of fashion in the body, in the plasmatic flows of energy rushing our excitement when our cognition is attuned to the expression and allure of another peer or the "object" of our cognition. *Fashion streams inside and between organisms in the excitation of emotional and plasmatic movements.*

Thus you know something is fashionable when it makes your body pulsate with desire, when your erotic emotion and imagination is intensified, and you feel the steam from the arousal of your sensibilities. You know something is fashionable when you can't tear your eyes off it, when it captures your sensibilities, anticipation and passion. At its best, fashion is more than a wearable signifier: it is a seamless alloplastic extension of pure flesh. Fashion is a prosthesis for orgastic potency, a technology of imagination, excitement and allure, making the human more god-like. As Freud famously argues;

"With every tool man is perfecting his own organs, whether motor or sensory, or is removing the limits of their functioning [...] Man has, as it were, become a prosthetic god. When he puts on all his auxiliary organs he is truly magnificent: but those organs have not grown on him and they still give him trouble at times." (Freud 1962: 42)

The prosthetic is both organic and social, and thus fashion does not happen in isolation, but is a heightened (or more "god-like") form of connection and interaction. Fashion is fundamentally a social phenomenon, a pulsation of energies coupling two bodies together. *Fashion is a form of flirting.* Enacted socially, it grabs attention and holds it: you know fashion works when you can't tear your eyes off its wearer. This attention excites and affirms the other, radiates a sense of attractiveness, sends a pulse of affection and pleasure. It is a co-creation between two people, a look of recognition and allure. At its best, fashion connects two people; it ties their attention together to form an emotional charge of attentive togetherness.[27] There is such a thing as a biosexual "sexual aura" or "sex appeal," which Reich sees as "the contact of two fields of orgonotic excitation." (Reich 1982: 7)[28]

Flirting in this sense should not be limited to the narrow experience leading up to sexual intercourse, but a much wider array of emotionally changed practices connecting the living bodies of organisms. Flirting is a series of practices, behaviors and rituals capturing the attention of a peer, drawing their sensory apparatus into an intimate world, inviting them to attune their sensations to each other in order to share an experience of anticipation.[29] Flirting is a *space of connection* in which passions are entwined; it is here fashion takes place.

In this way, fashion is a pure affirmation of life. In a connective expansion between two people, distance disappears. Two embodied minds touch and feel each other out. By enlarging the sensibilities of two bodies, fashion reawakens desire but does not necessarily imply a genital sexuality, even if, at its best, flirtation is like an electrical build-up of tension followed by discharge and relaxation in the gratification of mutually boosted self-esteem. Attention streams like a biological pulsation between two poles, two living organisms affirming an exchange of loving affect. This dynamic is much in tune with Spinoza's "conatus," that is, living organisms striving to persevere in being, a strive drawing them towards that which causes joy and avoiding that which produces pain. As a mutual gift, fashion is an affirmation of shared pleasure and joy, an open passage and exchange of attraction and attention, a streaming pulsation between two desiring bodies.

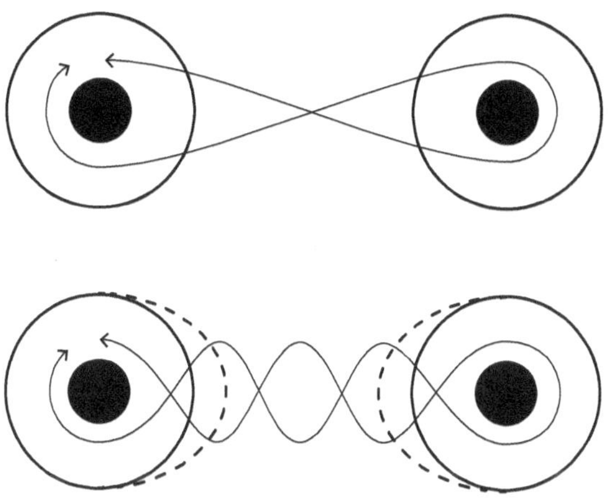

Top: two interacting orgonotic systems

Bottom: Two orgonotic systems engaged in flirting, expanding
towards each other in mutual plasmatic excitation

The process of orgone flow in fashion escalates in a series of steps. Firstly, the core of the organism expands from interest, reaching out towards the world and orienting itself towards others in an affirmative way. Secondly, as another organism opens itself, and the orgone orientations and cognitions of the two bodies catch each other, their streamings "feel each other out" to connect. The third stage of the affirming flirt is a co-joined streaming of bioelectrical affect, intertwining interests and pulses of affection that make the two organisms expand their worlds together. Thus the biosocial energy that affirms life, connecting two bodies to the currents of the time through healthy flirting and orgone streaming, is fashion.

If I have dressed up, and I feel at my best, I build up an excitation in the body, a willingness to be seen and be judged by my looks. Through my dressed sensorium, I reach out into the world and seek to touch the attention of others. Then, if someone gives me an affirming look or acknowledgment, I feel a rush of excitement, a release of tension, and pleasure rushes through my body. A passage has been opened between us. A build-up of excitation and then a wave of affirmation surges through my nerves from being seen and acknowledged. My neurons fire, dopamine rushes: I feel a sense of life affirmation, alive in my body in the most positive sense.

What a biosocial theory of fashion highlights is that garments act as vital interfaces, alloplastic extensions or prosthetics to the living organism; they are functionally integrated to the sensorial body. As such, they live through the excitement and expansion of the organism in search of pleasure, erotic enchantment, and orgastic potency. We search, touch, caress and capture our sensorial world through them, and we can of course also use them to reject others, regulating access to our attention. Yet fashion flows between us, moving our bodies. Like the excitation of the protoplasm, fashion is an affectual motility at the core of our being. Fashion design is the orchestration of these energies.[30]

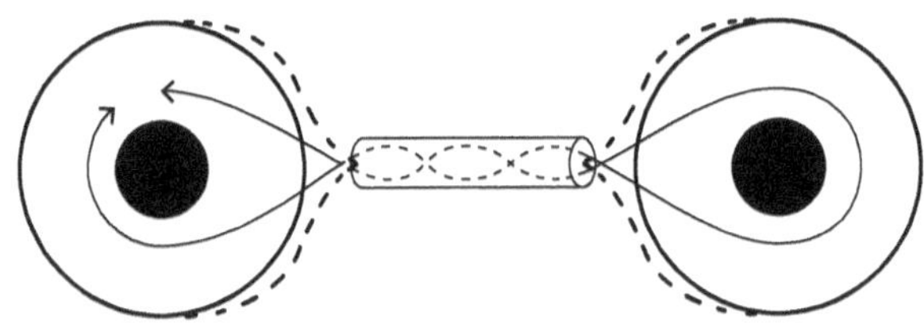

Flirting funneled through the narrow passage of fabricated commodities,
guiding but simultaneously limiting the expansion of orgonotic systems

However, fashion most often reaches consumers in the form of commodities. These commodities are the vectors or channels of energetic transmission. Our erotic vibrancy is materialized, packaged and funneled to consumers through the "system" of fashion, and it is in the interest of the industry this is done in ways that benefit the goals of this industry. We thus mistake trendy clothes with the energy of fashion. We see the incarnations of vitalist fashion as its true form, and we turn surprised each time we open the wardrobe and discover our recent purchases turn out to have lost their appeal and vibrancy and become dead forms even before the season is over.

In the following chapter, I will start the discussion by tying fashion to the protoplasmic and animal body of our being. Following Reich's argument, we are functionally analogous to primitive organisms, and I will argue also fashion is an extension of the sensorial and sexual elements of human being. In this sense, fashion is "feral," it is of the animal, more than merely a cultural or rational phenomenon. Even if the cultural industries and the "techniques of the self" attempt to domesticate, control and commoditize the forces of fashion, in essence fashion remains a living thing, always with the potential of breaking free of its commodity form.

However, as argued in the third chapter, fashion as a phenomenon is enacted in various social plays and dynamics. As we flirt and seek contact, we also are drawn into situations of rivalry, envy and social struggles.[31] Most of us come to seek the arms that the industry offers, what the industries or celebrities say is "in" or "out," that is, the industry manages to turn an abundance of vital energies streaming between bodies into scarce products trapped in a zero-sum game. For example, as children, we quickly learn the importance of looks and their workings of social dynamics, how in-group and out-groups dress and are judged. We learn that for every "in" someone has to be "out." Inclusion is something you buy, it is a look that joins the group, but simultaneously excludes others. We quickly become armored and fearful of being excluded, shamed and humiliated. To feel safer many consumers flee into the minimal excitement of "bare fashion" uniforms of jeans and t-shirts, mainstream suits or cheap and accessible fast fashion, securely judging others from the position of standing "outside" the social game. Others seek the shielded guidance of designers and influencers, desiring the emotional security of being led by oracles and powerful aesthetic dictates. These people are so armored, so fearful of social pain and emotionally rigid they willingly become slaves to the dictates of fashion. Or they become so dismissive and judgmental they sneer and snuff out every attempt on emotional communication, blaming the vital play of aesthetic sensuality as "shallow" or "feminine." Indeed, as pointed out by cultural historian Klaus Theweleit (1985), such fear of the organic and feminine is a core component of dominating masculine identity.[32]

As will be unpacked in the final chapter, the important lesson from a biosocial approach to fashion is its ability to challenge the commodity form promoted by the industry. In its energetic form, fashion is not limited to products but is a boundless aesthetic quest for excitement, potentially felt in each individual as a moment of expansion, opening, arousal, and an enlargement of sensibility. The locus of fashion is in your body, and potentially in all bodies, and it is not bound to gender, class, size, color, shape and age. We must come to realize fashion is not a thing, it is not bound to clothes or goods, but it is a place you go, an emotional space you enter inside yourself and another. Fashion is a pleasure, a feeling of growth in-between bodies. As with flirting, this emotion can be cultivated and shared abundantly as the important erotic endorsement it is.

Fashion is an energy. But be careful: those fetish heels are not symbols of penis envy, they are emotional exciters and highly charged orgone intensifiers!

FERAL FASHION

Fashion is of the animal, an uncontained living energy, joining the core of the organism to its environmental surroundings. Like every living thing and organic system it hungers for life, for contact, for nourishment, for procreation. Fashion is an intensification of living functioning. It extends the emotional and living processes of the organism, arousing the senses of itself and its peers. It is part of our experience, behavior and our living environment.

As will be outlined in this chapter, fashion is part of our living bodies, an extension of the organs sensing our living world. Furthermore, it is an extension of the organism, a sensory organ stretching beyond the confinement of the skin as flexible and sensual membrane between self and other. As noted earlier, this means fashion should not be confined to human culture and reason, as a language or system of signs handed down to us from the outside. Instead, we must see fashion as a dynamic process of coordination between the organism and its surrounding biosocial environment, what Jacob von Uexkull (2010) calls an *Umwelt*.

Fashion as a mode of continuous change is always striving to mobilize untamed affects, evoking non-conscious motilities of the body, attracting the body towards what philosophers Gilles Deleuze and Felix Guattari (1987) call "becoming-animal" – a continuous processes that turns away from the rational, predictive, stratified and cultured.[33] Becoming-animal turns fashion towards the non-human, the non-categorized, set free from cultural expectations, escaping singularity, overcoming the construction of identification and domestication.[34] It is feral in the sense of undomesticated, but also in the sense of being ferocious and predatory: it is uncontrollable, even though the fashion industry does its best to tame and package the living potentiality of fashion as a domestic force at the service of human beings. Clothes can be secure, predictable, stable, but fashion is always an unchecked intensity. Fashion is animated and always of the animal. That is to say, fashion is feral.

As Reich posits, in the very basic processes of life there is an expanding movement, the organism reaches outwards, opens up toward life and its peers, sensing the surrounding, in search for nourishment and sexual procreation. The flower opens up towards the light. The external membrane of the primitive organism, such as protoplasm, mollusk or jellyfish, expands from the core outwards, creating movement and sensorial contact with the world. Thus the natural plasmatic movements of the organism *"viewed in terms of function, [are] the same as those of living and swimming jellyfish."* (Reich 1973: 180)

> "Just as Darwin's theory deduces man's decent from the lower verte-brates on the basis of man's morphology, orgone biophysics traces man's *emotional* functions much further back to the forms of movement of the mollusks and the protozoa." (Reich 1973: 181)

The emotional functioning of the animal is present in the pulsating movement of the breath, opening and closing, in and out, an oscillation of life, of metabolism, the movement of a jellyfish in water. Life flows like electricity, in waves that build-up and then release. In pulsations of tension-relaxation, plus-minus, anticipation-gratification, life-death, in-out, inclusion-exclusion. As Reich (1982: 53) points out, human bodies are 70 percent water and we are basically fluid organic life forms. We are sexual jellyfishes, subsumed into the orgone oceans. To live in healthy streaming of orgonotic flows we must firstly come to recognize the element we are made up of, and let it stream unhindered.[35]

With his focus on energetic functioning, Reich takes a third position in-between the mechanism of the atomists and the mysticism of the idealists. His perspective is inspired by the similar positions of Aristotle and Driesch, and very much in line with the living struggle of life to sustain itself, that Spinoza called "conatus." Yet, even if Reich's perspective has many philosophical implications, his take on the organism is based in scientific empiricism with the aim of improving clinical practice and ultimately social reform. With its deep material and emotional entrenchment in its living surroundings (such as environment, social relationships and practices) Reich's ideas resonate well with the recent "affective turn" in social sciences. Here, bodies are not closed physiological or biological systems, but bodies and minds are radically open to the flows and passages of affect (Gregg & Seigworth 2010). Bodies are considered autopoietic, co-evolutionary, and symbiotic, in a continuous state of becoming and transformation, rather than stable and closed, ideas in line with the works of evolutionary biologists Lynn Margulis and Dorian Sagan (1986). Myra Hird (2010: 37) frames these relationships as "symbionts all the way down," that is, not only do affects transmit between individuals and move like waves through the social plasma, but organisms are "biomediated bodies," and matter is affective, from the scale of atoms up to societies and galaxies, a phenomenon Patricia Clough (2010: 210), calls "the affectivity of matter." Fashion brings matter and affect into an enclothed, biomediated and symbiont assemblage, as a full-spectrum "object of desire;" desired, and simultaneously imbued with agency of desiring and manipulating desires.

Fashion as a proto-sensorial and cognitive organic functioning is mirrored in other living processes. A motif recurrent in the singing of birds, the signaling tail of the peacock, the aesthetic arrangements of found colorful objects in the Bower bird. But we see similar expanding functioning in all mating rituals of animals; they reach out, touch and feel the sensorial extensions of the bodies. The sensation of emotional pleasure or joy is the primary intensity of fashion and the empirical principle of the subject's experience of being fashionable. The pleasure of agency in being seen, connected, affirmed, and bioelectrically charged with anticipation, is at the core of fashion.

The point of this argument is not to delineate a determinist position, limiting our interpretation of fashion to narrow evolutionary principles, but to tie fashion to the functioning of the plasmatic depths of the organic body. As Reich argues, living functioning echoes throughout the whole spectrum of organic life. Fashion is a transmitting extension of the plasmatic movements of the sensing body in its search for coupling with other organisms.[36] Even if living organisms are trapped in selective processes (and mating behaviors, posturings, flirtings are essential parts of this) we must not reduce it to *merely* this evolutionary process, but the aim is to unpack the emotional grounding of fashion in the living sensations of the organism, both in the body and socially, that is, *in biosocial being.*[37] However, embodiment is not something that takes place in isolation, but "intercorporeal," as Gail Weiss (1999: 5) highlights, "being embodied is never a private affair, but is always already mediated by our continual interactions with other human and non-human bodies." Fashion may flow from, in and through biological bodies, but is limitless in its capacity for unknown pleasures.

A person's "look" is both an inwards and outwards image, and as noted by Maurice Merleau-Ponty (1968: 255), "the flesh *is a mirror phenomenon* and the mirror is an extension of my relation with my body." The flesh of the body and the look are intertwined: I see my flesh and body in the mirror, but also, when I touch my flesh I am experiencing my sense of self through the lens of touching flesh. In both cases, I receive a "specular extract" (1968: 256) of myself. A look is an embodiment of our appearance, but it does not take place in a temporal vacuum, but in relation to a long history of experience we come to integrate into our emotional life. Fashion plays a central role in this social embodiment. We come to integrate the emotional state of our body in relation to our looks, what Brian Massumi (2002) terms "mirror vision," how the body feels is entangled with how it appears to our inner eye. In a similar vein, embodiment does not happen in social or cultural isolation, but we use images as references, or as a "prosthetic for imaginative work" as Mike Featherstone puts it (2010: 198). As part of human embodiment, we thus come to challenge and control our bodies in order to shape our sensory organs to the signals our social environment refracts back at us. This continuous exchange of looks and emotional cues resonates socially, bouncing between us, but also spoken within our biomediated bodies as "other voices" (Blackman 2012). Thus, even if the biological body is cultured in many ways, its living functioning is never fully domesticated, but part of its play is escaping, breaking off, swerving. I may experience some sense of fashion as I dress like my peers, but fashion is that little rule-breaking difference that makes all the difference emotionally, a sense of aliveness in the flesh. If we follow fashion journalist Suzanne Pagold's (2000: 8) definition, that fashion means "to look like everyone else, but before everyone else," fashion is that little "before" which makes my body shiver of desire, the little difference I use in flirtation.

The industry continuously tries to domesticate this flirting energy to its own ends, to manipulate, package and extract value from it. This *fabrication of fashion* means the harvesting, manipulation and packaging of living functioning, processing fashion into easily shipped and sold goods, not unlike the agribusiness. Journalist Michele Lee (2003) uses a similar homology between fast food and mass fashion, calling our everyday experience of cheap and accessible consumption a form of "McFashion." However, the full intensity of fashion cannot be reduced to this readily packaged and nutrition-free comfort food, but its potential as a living process and as energy is feral, it is connected to the foundational and natal potential of the living organism. Like other living processes, it strives to break free from constraints, to reproduce and expend itself, to connect the emotional and plasmatic movement of other living functionings. Like nature in the garden, the overflowing greens continuously overgrow the path, and fashion is in continuous expansion, nourished by social dynamics.[38] It is continuously escaping its master, always in a line of flight, struggling against territorialization, confinement, control and domestication. Fashion as a plasmatic energy is part of the process of becoming-animal, becoming-demon, becoming-feral. At its foundation, like flirting, it refuses to be held back by convention. Putting biosocial pulsation at the center of the experience of fashion (not the isolated garments) means to make desire and pleasure the primary intensity of fashion and the empirical principle for the subject's constitutional experience of being fashionable. Being fashionable in this sense does not mean being dressed in fashionable goods, but being in resonance with the plasmatic motility of being seen, being popular, being fluid, or in Reich's terms, being orgonotically charged. Fashion is thus not trapped within our heads, or in the cultural realm, but part of an expanded psychic and organic field. As Reich suggests, we must start by seeing how "the psychic apparatus is not psychological, but *biological.*" (Reich 1970: 116)

This biological placement means a shift in the locus of agency as well as the definition of fashion. It is not something happening is *out there*, in fabrication or in the *system* of fashion. We may utilize clothes in the process of flirting and appearances are part of the conjuring of the excitement. But the locus of agency, *where fashion happens*, is in the flirtatious motilities of our body, in the limitless living functioning breaking out of the body towards the world.

But flirting, like fashion and the feral, may all have a bad name, and needs to be given some nuancing. Popular author Alain de Botton takes aim at this in his essay "Why flirting matters," where he argues that we must not reduce flirting to the humiliating game of manipulative sexual affection, or reduce the attention of a potential partner to "only a flirt." Rather, "at its best, flirting can be a vital social process that generously lends us reassurance and freely redistributes confidence and self-esteem." Flirting breaks us out of our wounded state of loneliness,

> "Good flirting is in essence an attempt, driven by kindness and imaginative excitement, to inspire another person to believe more firmly in their own likability, psychological as much as physical. It is a gift offered not in order to manipulate, but out of pleasure at perceiving what is most attractive in another." (de Botton n.d.)

In culture which often highlights our own faults and failures to keep and achieve the cultural conventions of what is regarded as "sexiness," de Botton argues flirting "signals a willingness to use the imagination to locate what is most attractive about another person." Thus, flirting must not be reduced to a term of abuse, but an important enlargement of our social sensibilities. Flirting is an acknowledgment that "being recognized as erotically appealing is a hugely beneficial and ethical need of the soul" and such "erotic endorsement" must be liberated from its reduction to merely the genital act, "the tiny, difficult window of opportunity offered by an actual requirement to start to make love." De Botton calls for a liberation of flirting,

> "The ideal flirt is a pioneer in a crucial democratic science: they are attempting to correctly identify attractiveness in a way that will serve the many rather than the few. We should not only be grateful to good flirts; we should try to become good flirts ourselves." (de Botton n.d.)

Sexuality, passion, desire and vitality simultaneously inhabit the liminal space between biology and culture, flesh and spirit, anticipation and gratification. In the act of procreation our mortality is pushed towards immortality, and the present reaches out towards the future, even in the passionate denial of consequences. As Miriam DeCosta-Willis puts it,

> "Eroticism: The powerful life force within us from which springs desire and creativity and our deepest knowledge of the univierse. The life force that flows like an inscrutable tide through all things, linking man to woman, man to man, woman to woman, bird to flower, and flesh to

spirit. Our ancestors taught us this in their songs of love, their myths of creation, their celebrations of birth, and their rituals of initiation. Desire. Pleasure. Wholeness." (DeCosta-Willis, cited in Fuller 2008: 99)

The biosocial allures of flirting

Flirting must be understood beyond the narrow lens of "sexiness" and the very limiting promise of potential procreation. In a similar vein, we must also step beyond the everyday use of clothes and fashion to enact the "mirror-images" of what a "sexy" look is. If fashion is a form of flirting, it is so much more than pre-packaged sexiness and instead a rich play of sensation and attention. Flirting can point towards any biological or cultural signal used to shape resonance between plasmatic motilities. As de Botton suggests, we must see fashion as an art form, where clothes can evoke many affects and emotions, and which may

> "support a range of views about what it means to an interesting and desirable human being. In all its permutations, clothes make statements about values, ethics and psychological dispositions, and we judge them to be either 'beautiful' or 'ugly' depending on whether we approve or disapprove of the message they carry. To pronounce a certain outfit 'sexy' is not just to remark on the possibility that its wearer might be able to produce thriving children; it is also to acknowledge that we are turned on by the philosophy of existence it represents." (de Botton 2012: 45)

Reich's point of departure in biosocial functioning is the understanding that human emotions are grounded in biological processes, and from this we could see that also fashion has a biological substrate in the rich sense de Botton argues above. Surely, fashion is not merely a biological phenomenon, a promise of healthy offspring or territorial domination (seeking to mate Alphas), and neither does the function of arousal fully determine biological functions. But like the erotic imagination that is a fundamental part of flirting, fashion is more imaginative, alluring and intensive than mere biological mechanics in the crude sense.

The biological framing of emotions and the "stirring of emotions" through cultural practices is not isolated to the works of Reich, and much of the turn to affect in the social sciences over the last decades takes non-conscious emotional contagion as its point of departure when analyzing social phenomena. In many of these frameworks, affects flow as vital forces throughout the social realm, animating not only humans but also the relationships between humans and non-human entities. For example, feminist theorist Elizabeth Grosz (2008) points out that what we humans usually think of as our uniquely humanist practices, such as the arts, are not as cultured as we may come to believe. Not only do the arts exist amongst other organisms, but our human arts are also of the animal. According to Grosz, art is an extension and intensification of selection processes, emerging from the affirmation of life, the biological surplus energy surging through our species, as well as other non-human species. Grosz would probably agree that fashion is also such artistic affirmation of selective properties, an excessive force emerging from life itself, highly intensified in our evolutionary path, yet still parallel to most other living organisms (like the common example of the peacock as a morphological root to fashion and sexual selection). Art is part of our animal nature: "Art is of the animal. It comes, not from reason, recognition, intelligence, not from a uniquely human sensibility, or from any of man's higher accomplishments, but from something excessive, unpredictable, lowly" (Grosz 2008: 63). Fashion too is "of the animal" – it has a biological grounding in the feral living body and connects to the roots of our organism, to our social being. As Grosz posits,

> The haunting beauty of birdsong, the provocative performances of erotic display in primates, the attraction of insects to the perfume of plants are all in excess of mere survival [...] They attest to the artistic impact of sexual selection, the becoming-other that seduction entails. (Grosz 2008: 7)

Cognitive processes favor survival and produce mental modules that enact the erotic sensorium and its emotions. They can be callings, olfactory signals, dances and nestings, with each aesthetic act extending the animal territory. These acts play a central role in intraspecies mate selection, adaption and evolution. With elevated levels of testosterone, the feeling of lust arise and arousal exist along a continuum of intensity, which for humans range from sexual fantasies and looks, masturbation, courting, touches, all the way to intercourse. The regulation of intensity in these biological functions serves a central role in human culture; in rituals, protocols, customs and informal practices.

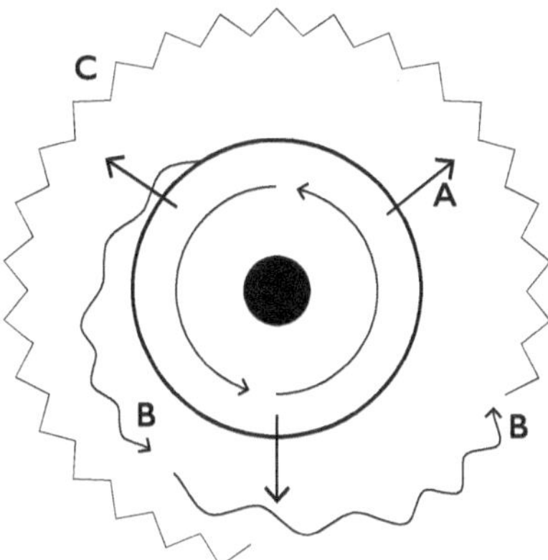

Markings (A) as an extension of the organism's living functioning, with each seductive or territorial act, such as a refrain of bird song (B), upholding the territorial boundary (C).

Putting fashion in relation to sexuality is a theme that echoes through the study of dress, not least the Freudian heritage in Flugel's erogenous zones of dress (1950), König's discussions on sexual exhibitionism (1973), Laver's exposition of the seduction principle (1969), or Steele's work of fetishism in fashion (1996). Also designers have been explicit in highlighting the sexual workings of their designs, such as John Galliano's statement about his designs,

> "I want people to forget about their electricity bills, their jobs, everything. It's fantasy time. My goal is really very simple: when a man looks at a woman wearing one of my dresses, I would like him basically to be saying to himself, 'I have to fuck her.'...I just think every woman deserves to be desired. Is that really asking too much?" (John Galliano, quoted in Bancroft 2012: 59)

Author Buzz Bissinger (2013) notices a relationship with fashion in tune with Galliano's statement, where the experience of encountering fashion is a strong embodiment of sexual desires beyond mere symbolism. In Bissinger's case, his passion is aroused by Gucci, "the pheromones of hot clothing defeat the part of the brain that rations rationality," and he continues,

> "I wanted the power that sex provides, all eyes wanting to fuck you and you knowing it, and both men's and women's clothing became my venue. [...] I love looking at myself in the mirror when I buy something new. I

love the sexual rush to the degree that I wonder if it has become a replacement for actual sex. But just like fucking, the magic of new clothing wears off quickly, and you can't resist the cravings for new purchases." (Bissinger 2013)

It may be obvious how Galliano's graphic note amplifies the industry's perspective on the biosocial usage of fashion in its reproduction of gender binaries, looks and sexual agency, and fashion modeling is continuously reproducing these affects in its play with anticipation, affects and arousal in order to promote commodities.[39] The industry is a place for fabrication and channeling of affects, and as Elizabeth Wissinger (2007: 251) argues, modeling is a "work that not only sells products, but also calibrates bodily affects, often in the form of attention, excitement, or interest." Evoking Bissinger's sexual rush, replacing actual sex itself, fashion modeling is one of many environments of affective labor where the model's precarious working condition is tied to the role of careful seducer, amplifying in and channeling affects to the emotional spectrum the look is meant to target. As Wissinger points to, "the modeling industry is organized to accommodate the unpredictable and volatile qualities of affective flow," (2007: 257) and as she shows,

> "Models work to stimulate interest in and attention to images by playing on forces that can consciously be perceived as desire, envy, or a need to belong (through being fashionable or 'in the know'); in so doing, they produce networks for affective flow that create community. They also, however, produce affective images, by tuning into a felt sense of vitality, aliveness, or engagement that takes no particular form, but taps into affective energy that is then conveyed via the virtual human contact of the image." (2007: 258)

Indeed, models in Wissinger's study are encouraged to show "'More energy!' 'Give it to me!' 'I've got to see the fire in your eyes!'" (2007: 259) Here, modelling becomes a cultivation and orchestration of affects in the service of fashion fabrication, yet it ties into a long history of cultural ritualizations of mating behavior.

As highlighted by biological anthropologist Helen Fisher (2004: 55), humans have throughout history cultivated a wide variety of rituals that cater to seduction. Eating is one of them, bringing potential partners together into close physical proximity, with food raising blood pressure and pulse rate, gestures articulating the body, with heightened levels of biological lust mixing social ritual with sexual excitement. In resonance with Fisher's observation of the rituals of eating, fashion similarly attunes sensual cognition, making appearance part of seduction. Yet even if fashion has a long history of social regulation and sumptuary laws, the seductive properties of fashion must not be tied down together with the confinement of sexuality to the familial secrecy of the bedroom. Even Freud ultimately locks up human sexuality in what feminist scholar Rosi Braidotti calls a "Fort Knox of the Libido" (2002: 140). For Freud, Braidotti argues, the animalist part in the libido keeps reproducing the boundaries of regulated binary State sexuality, even as Freud frames it as dangerous to civilization. In the Freudian view, even the liberation of the libido keeps reproducing the limitations of State sexuality. Take for example Carrie, one of the female characters in the popular iconic TV-series *Sex and the City*, who may have become an agent in the pursuit of their own pleasure, but as Frida Beckman argues, her striving towards orgasmic pleasure still iterates domesticated modes of what sexual pleasure is defined as culturally,

> "Carrie's orgasm and her disregard for her lover's pleasure indicate that even if feminist movements have achieved some development in terms of women's right to sexual pleasure, little has happened that would truly revolutionise what sexuality is about. The codes of the body are reconfigured only in so far as the clitoris gains a status similar to that of the penis. At the same time, the male characters, like many female characters through the history of representation, becomes little more than a set of sexualized attributes. For both female and male characters, then, the body remains a map inscribed by genital coding and patterns of power." (Beckman 2013: 107)

Sex and the City, which in many ways has become a token for an unapologetic extravaganza in binding fashion, sexiness and consumerism together, here also appears as a venue liberating as much as delimiting the imaginal space of what erotic dreams fashion can evoke. While celebrating many forms of alluring dress, and sometimes in a playful manner, the sexuality of the characters in the TV series never break out of the Fort Knox of the Libido, and similarly, their play with fashion never trespasses into the unknown or feral.

In contrast to this, an expansion of what "sexiness" is must also challenge the boundaries of State sexuality, and like eroticism always trespass into the unknown, other and uncanny. As Beckman posits, the "becoming demonic" part of erotic desire challenges the binary organization of sexes, to instead initiate new conjugated and indiscernible becomings, breaking apart gendered and genital coding. The "demonic" part is the ability to produce a thousand sexes and as many uncontrollable possible desires beyond the reproduction of the (male-oriented) orgasm. (Beckman 2013: 139)

> "Since Deleuze and Guattari aim to break with the reduction of sexual relations in terms of *the* father, *the* penis, *the* vagina' [...], it should also be logical to reconsider *the* orgasm. Why would the orgasm not harbour multiplicity—a thousand tiny orgasms, a pack multiplicity that howls and runs with the pack that is the body without organs? [...] We need to allow the many wolves to enter the sexual body. We need to allow for pack orgasms. One or many wolves? ask Deleuze and Guattari. Similarly I ask: One or many orgasms?" (Beckman 2013: 143)

Similarly, Beckman argues, the orgasm must not be seen as a reproductive discharge limited to the amorous machine, or an endpoint or climax, but more as a multi-faceted attractor of one of many lines of desire. Thus the orgasm has very little to do with the individual subject and the organism called its body, but instead it exceeds the limits of the subject and makes desire and pleasure available as a continually mutating force. At its most extreme, it could be a force flowing in all directions and along all routes. Similarly, the desire of fashion must be seen beyond the binary between the biological and the cultural, masculine and feminine, sexual and phantastic, or body and imagination. Instead these instances exist on a continuum and between various states of prosthetic and alloplastic assemblages.[40] In resonance with French author Stendhal's famous statement that "beauty is the promise of happiness," also fashion is a promise of pleasure, or one or many forms of sensorial excitement pointing towards one or many processes of bliss, one or many (be)comings. With a multitude of desires, genders, sexes and forms of comings, we must see how the function(s) of the orgasm(s) as the promises of fashion are themselves multiplying beyond the realm of the narrow pleasures of genital sexual acts into a pack of positive valence, arousals and fetishes. The ferality of this type of sexuality is much like the Internet meme Rule 34 suggests, "if it is conceivable, there is porn of it - no exceptions."

As noted earlier, the flirting of fashion is so much more than its associations to sexiness. Whereas Reich's focus on the orgasm is modeled on a normative male experience, and sexiness as primarily a feminine trait, this perspective must be complemented with a rich variety of sensorial arousals beyond binaries and dispositions.[41] Fashion as a form of flirting taps into a rich spectrum of colors, genders, proportions, dreams, passions, in a rich process of continuously emerging biosemiotic causation, or "semiogenesis" (Tonnesen 2012). Such process may be a central part of the varieties and selective properties of fashion change; to continuously open new vistas for social plasmatic motility. Yet it also mobilizes a realm of the imaginal and phantastic, the intensity of anticipation and frissons, that is, the dark sorcery of the erotic realm and the unknown pleasures that entails.

Flirting's merger of phantasy and biosemiosis includes an embrace of the carnal knowledge inherent in fashion, exuding charismatic self-assertion: prestige, vanity, adoration, and rage. It expresses and affirms intimate social bonds, but also promises the pleasures of violating them. Erotic agency *does* things with us: it animates and pulls us towards achieving supreme sensual gratification. Similarly, fashion plays a key part in the everyday cultural intensification of such biosocial functions, evoking anticipation and excitement. Eroticism thus mobilizes a rich array of our sensorium, and fashion does too, from the visual arousal to olfactory sensualities, from the touch of velvet to the psychoacoustic clapper of heels or rustling of fabrics (cf. Cho *et al* 2001; Zwicker & Fastle 2007). When fashion works at its best, it arouses our sensorium and promises erotic motility; looks of course, but also touch, sound, smell, weight, posture, and pressures on the skin, moblilizing phantasies and imaginal images of the flesh, affirming the vital and affective properties of the body, the intensification of passion.

To Grosz, the pleasures of affect, sensation and intensities of sexuality emerge from chaos, and it is from here art extracts its qualities of sensual signification. As Grosz has it, sexual intensities give shape to artistic qualities, as they are essentially expressive. As with so many other animals, the pleasure of life pulsates through human action, where sexual interaction becomes art as its beauty is of no use other than seduction itself; "the frivolous, the unnecessary, the pleasing, the sensory for their own sake" (Grosz 2008: 7) It recognizes the organism as a "vibratory being" where sexuality functions as a "bodily intensification" as "vibration, waves, oscillations, resonances affect living bodies, not for any higher purpose but for pleasure alone" (Grosz 2008: 33) Much in tune with Reich's ideas, Grosz argues how life vibrates of desiring bodies, as these

> "rhythms of seduction, copulation, birth, death—coupled with those of the earth—seasons, tides, temperatures—are the conditions of the refrain, which encapsulates and abstracts these rhythmic of vibratory forces into a sonorous emblem, a composed rhythm" (Grosz 2008: 55).

Fashion is one such artistic expression, emerging not from culture but from our biological search for emotional motility, as plasmatic rhythms and waves rush between us, through our coupled orgontic fields.

Fashionallaxis and biosocial coupling

So far, the biosociality of fashion motility discussed above has primarily engaged the arousal of the body and potential mates or peers. But biosociality opens new vistas for the larger social body, how the waves of positive valence can stream throughout the larger populations in resonance with the time, or the aesthetic *Zeitgeist*. As Grosz (2008) mentions earlier, the chaos of nature is not unstructured, but organized though various forms of evolutionary couplings. Unpacking such couplings may help us move beyond seeking an inherent meaning in fashion. This is also in resonance with Reich's perspective, as he posits, "the living merely functions. It does not have 'meaning.'" (Reich 1976: 104)

Here, Reich's perspective is in tune with more contemporary biology and cognitive philosophy. Biologists such as Humberto Maturana and Francisco Varela point toward how complex communication is not uniquely a human phenomenon, but that multisensory coordination of behavior is common across the animal realm. Many examples of such behavior overlap with human abilities, and can also tell us much about the functionality of signals and coordination between organisms, effects we often miss as we seek the "meaning" inherent in communication. As Maturana and Varela posit, an ant colony forms a superorganism through the whole colony's shared cognitive system, joined by the "chemical coupling" between every ant in a "continuous chemical flow" of *trophallaxis* (Greek 'flow of foods'), or the flow of chemical secretions between the members of the colony (Maturana & Varela 1992: 186). To Maturana and Varela every living system is a cognitive system, and life itself is a process of cognition, reflexive feedback control, and inter-operation with the surrounding world.

> "There is no 'transmitted information' in communication. Communication takes place each time there is behavioral coordination in a realm of structural coupling." (Maturana & Varela 1992: 196)

It is the couplings and not the isolated agency of the individual ants that make up the colony, or to use Reich's terminology, the living functioning of the colony is not isolated in atomic ants, but in the relationships that affect the overall plasmatic motility of the colony. The ant colony, with its distributed cognitive system, makes up a superorganism, and it is the interconnectedness between individual ants that creates a responsive dynamic, which far outreaches that of the individual ant. To put focus on the cognitive qualities of the colony, Maturana and Varela argue that the ants do not communicate "something." Rather, their coordination is an integral part of the cognitive act itself. The colony is coupled directly through its cognitive sensibility to the environmental dynamics in its proximity. The very act of *knowing*, that for Maturana and Varela is the same as *doing*, "brings forth a world" (Maturana & Varela 1992: 234). The cognitive act of sensing is what couples organisms and environments together; meaning, *knowing* and *doing* are not distinct parts of the cognitive process but one interacting whole.

Cognition and the environment stand in a contrapuntal relationship. This contrapuntal connection is similar to how Varela and Maturana see the "structural coupling" between organism and environment, which is in turn essential to *autopoiesis*, the systemic process of a living system reproducing and maintaining itself.[42] An organism is "organized" as a set of relationships, existing between components, not within the properties of the components themselves. As Maturana puts it,

A cognitive system is a system whose organization defines a domain of interactions in which it can act with relevance to the maintenance of itself, and the process of cognition is the actual (inductive) acting or behaving in this domain. *Living systems are cognitive systems, and living as a process is a process of cognition.* This statement is valid for all organisms, with and without a nervous system. (Maturana 1980: 13)

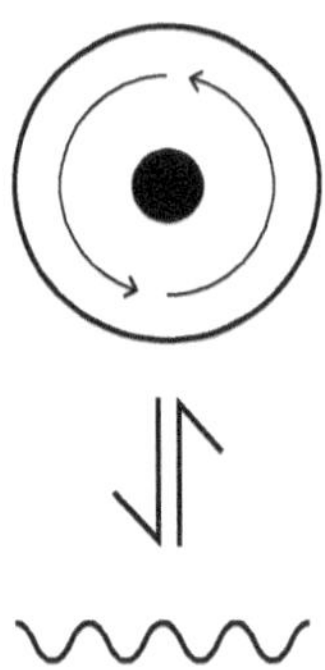

An organism as autopoietic system (continuous self-reproducing metabolic dynamics within boundary membrane), coupled to its environment

As such cognitive biosemiotic processes displace an anthropocentric perspective on language and meaning, they also expose what is different between animal and human use of language. As Bains argues,

Animals use signs and communicate, but they do not live *in* language and do not grasp imperceptible sign relations as such. [...] Or to be more reversed, we can say that currently we have no knowledge of a non-human *linguistic* animal that ipso facto grasps (or rather understands) the incorporeal sign relations as distinct from its terms. (Bains 2006: 70f)

From the ant colony's collective, the act of cognition adjusts its *doings,* and the anthill, the external architecture built collectively as an extended phenotype, becomes *part of its genetic and evolutionary body* (Dawkins 1982). Thus the extended body with its tools and prosthetics is not uniquely human phenomenon. As already noticed by William James,

"a man's Self is the sum total of all that he can call his, not only his boy and his psychic powers, but his clothes and his house, his wife and children, his ancestors and friends, his reputation and works, his lands, and yacht and bank-account. All these things give him the same emotions. If they wax and prosper, he feels triumphant; if they dwindle and die away, he feels cast down, not necessarily in the same degree for each thing, but in much the same way for all" (James 1890: 291f)

Here, James is in deep correspondence with Reich's plasmatic motility of emotion and remotion, of how the organism expands and shrinks both emotionally, biologically and socially with its relationships to its surroundings. The extended body integrates with its alloplastic tools and prosthetics, relationships and cultural signifiers, living coupled with its biosemiotic environment with membranes, appendages and organs cognitive of its situatedness.[43]

This type of extended cognition, merged with the agency and doings of the organism, is what Maturana calls our *bodyhood*, our physiological state of existence. Our bodyhood is not a container of ourselves, but the extended sensory vehicle with which we operate in the world, our tactile realm of perception. Here, the whole body is an organ attuned to our surroundings and it also affects our surroundings. We modulate the world through our bodyhood, our interactions, and our skills—*what our body can do*. Our bodyhood extends into the world together with our skills and tools. As an organism crawls, digs, swims or flies, elements open to its doings, just like sharpened senses makes different environments perceivable, such as sounds, smells, and how night vision makes the dark maneuverable for the organism. According to Maturana:

> Bodyhood and manner of operating as a totality are intrinsically dynamically interlaced; so that none is possible without the other, and both modulate each other in the flow of living. The body becomes according to the manner the living system (organism) operates as a whole, and the manner the organism operates as a whole depends on the way the bodyhood operates. (Maturana 1997)

Among social insects, structural coupling occurs through the chemical coupling of trophallaxis. As Maturana and Varela posits, "There is a continuous flow of secretions between the members of an ant colony through sharing of stomach contents each time they meet" (Maturana & Varela 1987: 186). Coordination happens through the chemical functions of coupling between organisms. As Bains posits, "this results in the distribution throughout the colony of substances (e.g., hormones) that determine the differentiation and specification of roles. For example, the queen is only a queen as long as she is fed in a certain way. This is also the case for 'barren females,' 'worker females,' 'males,' and so on." (Bains 2006: 106f)

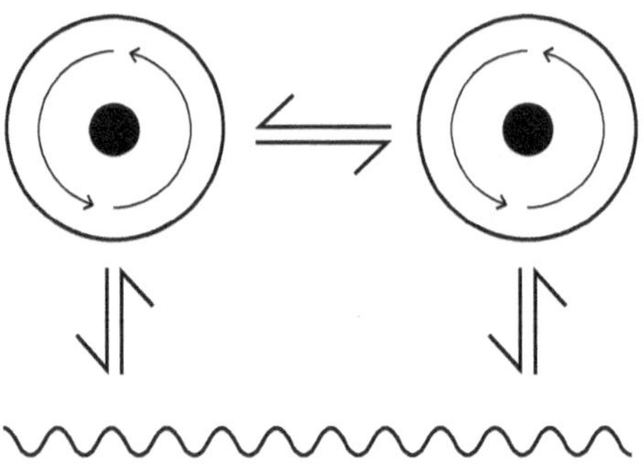

Two (or more) organisms in recurrent interactions with environment and each other, leading to structural congruence and second-order structural coupling (socio-functional coordination)

Bains draws analogies to the same principles amongst larger organisms, with more complex nervous systems, which allows for greater flexibility, "For example, a wolf pack, whose members coordinate their behavior by adopting different postures, can hunt and kill a larger moose; a singe wolf could not do this." (Bains 2006: 107) Similarly, the dynamic between the pack and pray is fused into the evolutionary phylum of both wolf and moose, and this in turn also affects the surrounding environment and growth, a term referenced as an "ecology of fear" (Ripple & Beschta 2004).

The same principle of behavioral coordination runs through other forms of interaction between organisms whereby organisms coordinate their behavior by means of olfactory, visual, auditory, and chemical secretions, especially in organisms with a rich nervous system. This is why Maturana and Varela (1992: 211ff) coin the term "linguallaxis" as a linguistic parallel to trophallaxis, referring to the coupling in language between human beings. Here, language is an *act* of coordination between beings, rather than a representation or symbolic entity external from them, thus language becomes what they call *languaging,* a continuous flow of interactions that produce the *coordination of coordinations of actions.*[44]

As two embodied minds touch and feel each other out, we experience the organic "knowledging" and "languaging" that Maturana and Varela places at the center of interacting organisms. It is a phenomenon recurring all the way from the simplest symbiotic relationships, in protozoans, ants, schools of fish and flocks of mammals, to the more complex human societies. Drawing parallels to the flirting function of fashion, it is a way the human organism extends into the world, reaches out to couple sensuous affects with other humans, evoking allure and imagination. In that way fashion is an affirmation, an expansion and "yes" of life, the same force that pushes an organism into growing, seeking light and nourishment, which in turn makes Reich's perspective on the biological and metabolic foundation of philosophy in line with that of philosopher Hans Jonas (1992). For human beings, this nourishment is social affirmation. In a connective expansion between two people, distance disappears and their worlds grow and expand, and as relational theorists Arthur Aron and Elaine Aron (1986) notice, this builds on the "fundamental human motivation [which is] to enhance potential self efficacy," where our desire for interpersonal relationships is the cognition of self-development through interpersonal expansion. Attention streams like a biological pulsation between two poles, with flirting as an open passage and exchange of affirmation, a streaming pulsation between sensual and desiring bodies. This is where one can see how fashion is always a social event, it always connects people, in one way or another. Per definition, fashion cannot be experienced alone. Thus fashion takes on a special form of languaging and "linguallaxis" to become what we should call "fashionallaxis"– *the energetic and coupled exchange of behavioral coordination through ephemeral extended sensibilities (temporal aesthetics) between living organisms.*

Such an approach highlights other parts of fashion interactions, than the macro-perspectives on fashion, where fashion is primarily seen as a language and semiotic communication system merely using bodies and identities to signal the aesthetic trends of the times. It thus anchors the works of Thorstein Veblen (1899) and Georg Simmel (1957), or in the more contemporary works of Roland Barthes (1983), Alison Lurie (1981) and Malcolm Barnard (1996) to the emotional core of the living organism. This emotional and material grounding in the body also adds a biological point of view to the perspectives that frame fashion as a tool for "identity-production-as-project", for example in the works of Anthony Giddens (1992), which place the body as a container for exposing the mixed-and-matched self. Or rather, the container is more of a membrane, a bladder, a flexible sensory organ the organism uses to touch as feel the surrounding through the process of fashionallaxis.

Fashionallaxis is a biosocial semiogenesis, a living process of semiotic causation, it is a materialist perspective on how fashion acts between peers, a non-conscious and chaotic process of flirting which puts emphasis on coordinated biological behaviors more than cultural meanings or traditions of dress. Fashion is not out there, but in the process of fashionallaxis, in a continuous mode of creation and becoming (like Simmel would have it), and it gains its role in the coordination of flirting behaviors. However, even if the locus of agency in the process of fashionallaxis lies in the coupling between organisms and the energetic flow between them, this does not mean the process happens in a vacuum; the organisms are coupled to their environment (and to each other). Coupling always takes place within a milieu to which the organisms themselves have adapted their cognitive behaviors towards. This environment is in biosemiotics called the organism's *Umwelt*.

An *Umwelt* of fashion

According to ethologist Jakob von Uexkull, every organism lives within an *Umwelt*, a species-specific world, which is coupled to its sensory organs and cognitive processes. Uexkull is cited at many places in Reich's work, and there is a close affinity between their two approaches to their subjects. Similarly, they both think across levels of metaphor into material and objective biological functionings. Examining Uexkull's ideas of the coupling between organism and environment highlights how the distinction between self and other is much more fluid than we might usually think, and how our organs are attuned to the environment they are part of, thus transmitting the motility between the organic plasma and the world. Organs are coupled to their symbiont, like the orchid and wasp, the mouth and nipple, as in the examples given by Deleuze and Guattari (1987).

The *Umwelt* (German "environment") is neither objective nor subjective, in terms of the traditional modern dichotomy, but is entangled in a triadic relationship between the sign, organism and its world. This triad has three essential components; the organism experiencing, the object experienced, and the biologic sign relation by which the object exists as experienced, thus intertwining the world with the organism's reflexes and behaviors. The world is not "out there", exposed in its fullness, but instead the Umwelt is "called forth" by our senses, not too unlike how we use metaphors in language to frame and "see" certain abstract concepts (Wheeler 2006:24). However, whereas the metaphor exists purely in our mind, the Umwelt is a material coupling between the world and the organism's operational behavior. Seeing fashion as situated within an Umwelt helps us see one of its key characteristics: it is not something you wear, but *fashion is a space you enter*, an emotional sphere of flirting where biosocial energies pulsate in conjunction with anticipation and imagination. This space is the Umwelt of fashion; simultaneously material, social and imaginal.

As suggested by semiotician John Deely (1986), experience is a pattern of inherently imperceptible yet objective relations and to understand a being is to understand a field of relations within its being-in-the-world, its Umwelt.

> If we are now to translate *Umwelt* as objective world, we are in a fair position to see the significance of this notion for the understanding of semiosis as a unique process in nature. An *Umwelt*, von Uexkull tells us, is the physical environment as filtered or transformed by the given organism according to what is important or 'significant' to it. Elements of the physical environment are networked objectively, i.e., so as to establish the sphere of experience as something superordinate to and strictly transcending, all the while containing partially and resting upon aspects of, the physical environment in its 'natural' or 'mind-independent' being. *Umwelten* are thus species-specific: No two types of organisms live in the same objective worlds, even though they share the same physical environment. What the bat seeks (nourishment) the moth avoids (providing nourishment for bats), and conversely. (Deely 1986: 269)

The Umwelt is an objective world and a "semiotic reality" for the beings sharing it. To Uexkull, the Umwelt is a sphere of perceptive cues surrounding the organism, full of significant signs that it alone knows, a cognitive sphere containing the self-world. The size of the sensorial sphere stretches as far as the organism's organs can reach out and capture the surrounding signs. As the organism moves through the environment a real world comes into objective being (Uexkull 2010: 43). This makes Uexkull argue sense organs and effector organs may be the same in lower organisms. The organs answer to tactile responses. Also, sensorial organs are coupled to their signs in their Umwelt. Nervous and muscular bundles correspond to qualities in the Umwelt, and each species has sense organs relevant to their Umwelt. For more complex animals the sense and effector organs overlap and limbs become less specific to grasp more complex environments. For humans, speech makes it possible to become independent from the causal presence of objects, and also adds temporal framing of future and past, which becomes key components in human learning and being (Brentari 2015: 89ff).

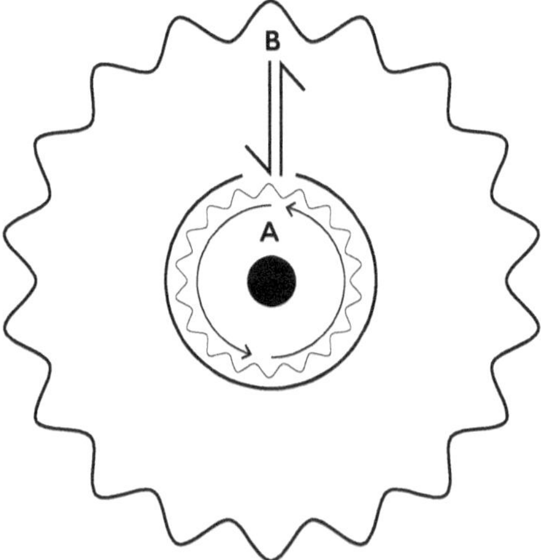

Organism with structural coupling between Innenwelt (A) and surrounding Umwelt (B), inserting the organism into its living environment through contrapuntal mirroring

Thus, as Uexkull highlights, the development of the organism is coupled to its Umwelt in a contrapuntal manner, and these two connected environments evolve together. The Umwelt is mirrored by the organism's corresponding *Innenwelt*, or inner world, which is not merely psychological but physiological: it is the sensory and nervous system that connects to the Umwelt, applying biological signs according to a their interconnection, or *Bauplan*, "building plan." This plan is the "overall organization of the environment-animal system" where the organism's behavior is matched with its Umwelt (Brentari 2015: 77). The organism matches the Umwelt by a process of insertion (*Einpassung*), as a complement to mere adaption (*Anpassung*): integration between worlds in reciprocal dependence. The bee corresponds to the flower, and flower to the bee, the hunter to the hunted, and hunted to the hunter. Similarly, the spider's web corresponds to the fly, even though the individual spider may never have seen a fly: the web is still a faithful portrait of the "primal fly." (Uexkull 2010: 158f) My *Innenwelt* of fashion is my organic grounding, of how my experiences of life have constructed my emotions, how my surrounding has inserted itself in me, and it mirrors my Umwelt.[45]

It is important to see how well Uexkull fits into Reich's ideas as political theorist as he connects biosocial processes with social situations beyond Freud's narrow scope of the immediate family (the Mother and Father). To Reich, the social landscape, with its class relations, socio-economic resources, ideologies, customs and laws, plays a more important role in shaping the living functioning of the organism than more abstract concepts like the Oedipal drama. A person's energetic functioning depends on social conditions and constraints, environments such as education and upbringing, attitudes towards sexuality in society, and repression and relationships to authoritarianism, or the "mass-psychology." (Reich 1946) The human social organism's interaction with its Umwelt comes to stand in a central position in Reich's ideas; the organ sensation of an armored individual stands in relation to the repressive tendencies and material means in the social environment.[46] This means wider social and sexual reform need to happen throughout society to prevent neurosis and schizophrenia, a social reconstitution of ideas, values and practices Reich (1945) calls the "sexual revolution."

Thus the Umwelt of fashion plays a key role in the formation of plasmatic functionings and how flirting as an energy can be enacted on a wider social scale. Uniforms may be a classic example of institutions doing their best to control the Umwelt of dress, limit individual expression (yet simultaneously triggering new erotic dimensions and allures). School uniforms may serve such de-individualizing purpose, expressing belonging while trying to limit aesthetic peer competition. But as most know having grown up with them, they still offer many variables of expression and continuous challenges for users to manipulate the application of the rules, adding adornments, adjusting hems, moving buttons. Authoritarian regimes may limit the accessibility to certain expressions, or promote local variations, such as in the Eastern block in Soviet times. Similarly, certain cultures and traditions try to minimize the most explicit potential for flirting and expressions of sexiness, for example in the "modest clothing" of religious communities. But it would be a mistake to think that flirting or fashion does not happen in such settings, even if some expressions are limited. Rather, other sensoria and biosemiotic signs are developed in details and gestures. The energy still finds ways, bypassing blockages or going through the cracks.

The opposite may be Umwelts where flirting is an essential part of the environment, for example in nightclubs where the space layout is constructed to make looking part of the experience, in mirrors, lights, elevations etc. Similarly, the crowd drawn to a certain club may ravel in expressiveness and sensuality and where the movement of the body is an explicit form of mating and of challenging boundaries. Obscure signs and signals (often irrelevant outside the club) bind attention, anticipation and behaviors together into site-specific fashionallaxis. Many nightclubs are Umwelts open for emotional experiments where people can "come out" and grow as emotive beings, "letting off steam," testing personas, or search their plasmatic depths in conjunction with others. However, this does not mean all such environments are more inclusive per definition; instead, each Umwelt attunes its own fashionallaxis and its own possibilities for emotive couplings.

Yet the Umwelt is not merely material. We must pay attention to the psychopolitical settings of the fashion Umwelt and how the imaginal aspects of it are constrained, not least through adaptations to peer pressure. Fashion and flirting are not guaranteed continuous affirmations, but are always at the risk of rejection, denial and possibly public rebuttal and the following social pain, and this modulates what we imagine as possible ways to dress. Even dreams are touched by the judgment of peers and friends; what identities are popular or marginalized, the dynamics of who is "in" and who is "out," and how the dread of shame and humiliation translates into an anxious or even fearful relationship to what we aspire to be. Such discomfort often results in a denial of not only fashion but also the body, where the wearer tries to escape judgment through the use of uniforms ("bare fashion" like suits or jeans) or low-risk fashion ("fast fashion") in order to "go under the radar" of their peers.

Such dynamics, between pleasure and pain, affirmation and anxiety, "in" and "out," are an environment the fashion industry thrives in; where consumers keep on buying to just keep up with their peers in a continuous fear of sinking, as a *perpetuum mobile* (Bauman 2010). In such an Umwelt, the industry fabricates a scarcity of flirting, making users dependent on and addicted to fashionable goods, rather than cultivating an abundance of energies.

Look in the mirror. The face that pins you with its double gaze reveals a chastening secret: You are looking into a predator's eyes. Most predators have eyes set right on the front of their heads, so they can use binocular vision to sight and track their prey. Our eyes have separate mechanisms that gather the light, pick out an important or novel image, focus it precisely, pinpoint it in space, and follow it; they work like top-flight stereoscopic binoculars. Prey, on the other hand, have eyes at the sides of their heads, because what they really need is peripheral vision, so they can tell when something is sneaking up behind them. Something like us.

Diane Ackerman (1990: 229)

SCARCITY AND REALIST FASHION

Most of us have had this or similar experience: an outfit that works perfectly in one setting is a disaster in another context. It may be "too much," "too little," or plainly wrong. An outfit that may make us feel perfectly right and on top of things at the nightclub may make us feel vulnerable on public transport going back home. From having gotten the right kind of looks earlier in the evening, now the clothes turn me into prey and my flight-instincts fire. But the paradox is apparent: the outfit that boosted my confidence and got me past the bouncer is the same that later makes me feel defenceless. Other people control the settings in which I enact fashion, often with radically different agendas than my own: the Umwelt in which I engage in fashionallaxis changes and it echoes into my emotional depths.

The transitions between environments and contexts set off a clash of expectations. The nightclub is no charity, it profits from the money and energy I spend there, and it is framed by institutional interests. It is the bouncer's job to make it prestigious, to attract the happy, rich, beautiful (and not too drunk), while keeping the losers out. It is the exclusivity of the club, where I can feel I play fashion with the peers I desire to be with. At the nightclub the fashion distinction between "in" and "out" takes on social and spatial dimensions, which strikes deep into the emotional depths of those desiring to be there.

The energy of fashion is not transmitted equally everywhere, but is situated in stratified environments. Some have more agency than others, and some have more developed organ sensation to environments of prestige. Our embodied energy of fashion is processed through a *vectorial* social and institutional dynamic, what we may call a "power-grid." This concept puts the spotlight on how there are infrastructures and territories through which fashion is processed as an energy, how it is regulated and guided in certain directions. The example of the bouncer makes it apparent how my flirting at the nightclub is orchestrated through the arrangement of the guest list, the protocol of the bouncer, the prestige of the DJ, the layout of the space, and of course the location and prices. Similarly, the way I dress at work reflects the hierarchies of my work place, and affects how I can play with the living energies of my body within this hierarchy. The power-grid highlights how the biosocial energies are not enacted across a level playing field, but channelled through already existing relationships and ideologies.

But most importantly, a power-grid takes material shape as vectors restrict the accessibility of the tools and prosthetics I utilize in the act of flirting. Brands, shops, prizes and wait lists sort and stratify who can access what objects and who has access to the places where flirting matters more; the "right" places. For the elite to keep its exclusive place, it needs to be restrictive and exclude those aspiring to replace them. As pointed out sociologist Robert Faris (2012) while it may be nice to have many friends and this may make you popular, it is more important to be picky with relationships if you want to ascend the social ladder, you need to have the "right" friends, and keep them for yourself: upholding scarcity is the key component for social status.

The power-grid of social relationships is deeply dependent on *collaborateurs* or collaborationists, that participants not only play along, but *desire* to be part of the game in their struggle to ascend, and their desires are essential in the enforcement of regulation and repression onto others. By hijacking the living functioning of fashion and amplifying human tendencies of pride, envy and rivalry into the social dynamics of fashion, the industry manages to lure peers to enforce its dictates onto each other, thus reaching into the living emotional functionings of everyday people. Peers start to judge each other by what is considered "in" or "out" and manifest such distinctions spatially and socially through in-groups and out-groups, looks of belonging and the very means of identity production.

Fashion and flirting are energies that break through social conventions and move across social boundaries, across classes and contracts, so it is no surprise flirting is such a controversial social practice. The energy of flirting is always a "stolen look," attention captured in a way that may cause disruption; it can cut across social conventions, bonds and boundaries.[47] Likewise, love and mating are dangerous passions. This is not only because they are matters of attraction and seduction, but like every selection, they make explicit distinctions between losers and winners. As David Buss argues, human mating behavior is an activity imbued with nature but also most heavily controlled by culture, in rituals and laws. And mating is not only an affair of pleasure, as "efforts to attract mates often backfire. Conflicts erupt within couples, producing downward spirals of blame and despair." (Buss 1994: 1) Indeed, as Buss suggests, passions are threatening to the order of things, as they break with the rational mind, upend conventions and social agreements. The motility of love is one of such "dangerous passions,"

> "Each of us owes our existence to thousands of generations of successful ancestors. As their descendants, we have inherited the passions that led to their success—passions that drive us, often blindly, through a lifelong journey in the struggle for survival, the pursuit of position, and the search for relationships." (Buss 2000: 1)

As Buss highlights, passions are the fruits of joy and life, but also carry much grief and a special supreme sensibility as jealousy balances seduction and competition within the realm of relationships and love.

> "The drives that stir us out of bed at dawn and hurl us headlong into our daily struggles have two sides. On the positive side, passions inspire us to achieve life's goals. They impel us to satisfy our desire for sex, our yearning for prestige, and our quest for love. [...] But the passions carry a darker, more sinister side. The same passions that inspire us with love can lead to the disastrous choice of a mate, the desperation of unrequited obsession, or the terror of stalking. Jealousy can keep a couple committed or drive a man to savagely beat his wife." (Buss 2000: 2)

While we may think of biological processes such as sexual or natural selection as almost mechanical, it is the passions that animate them to become the foundations of evolution. Similarly, selection has losers and winners, making the process far from a game. Aggression and territoriality take different evolutionary lines and intensities, where dragonflies may attack intruders by darting at them, others use vocal signaling, such as bird song, or odors, such as urine, to demarcate the boundaries of their territories. Thus, as Edward Wilson highlights in his work on sociobiology, the techniques of repulsing competitors and predators "can be as explicit as a precipitous all-out attack or as subtle as the deposit of a chemical secretion at a scent post." (Wilson 1975: 256) Here too, fear and anger play central roles, as fear gives rise to a long lasting "appraisal and coping style that focuses on the threats and loss of status in a hostile and competitive world." (Plutchik 2003: 322) Furthermore, the continuum from the subtle biochemical signal or gesture to the all-out attack is elaborated and enhanced through culture. Here, even the faintest signal may translate to a physical state, as the "threat to one's self-concept, one's integrity, or one's psychological well-being can elicit fear, and such threats are rarely eliminated by physically running away." (Izard & Ackerman 2000: 260) Thus, in the human animal, protecting self-esteem and self-concept is done through cultural territories and signifiers, both through loyalty and conformity to the group, or through new alliances and practices. The passions may uphold such alliances, but may in other situations undermine them, as in the classic example of falling in love with the enemy where two passions clash against each other.

Clothing is an extension of our passions. Our clothes form alloplastic assemblages with the organism and could be studied from a biological perspective, rather than as anthropocentric artifacts in alignment with cultural techniques. From a perspective of biosocial fashion, the task is to trace the way these artifacts work in conjunction with the body's energetic and plasmatic functions. This however does not mean cultural and social processes do not affect the biological dynamics of fashion, but rather, our emotional responses to the workings of fashion in our body are very much learned from experience. As neuroscientist Lisa Feldman Barrett (2017) argues, emotions are constructed, not fetched from some deep generic bank inside the human DNA. The workings of, for example, pleasure or fear on our bodies are highly individual, depending on our culture or experiences. Also Reich points out, character structure and armoring is a *congealed* social process and thus our experience of fashion and flirting is dependent on the dynamics and couplings in our Umwelt – and certain social fabrications and power-grids influence these processes of congealment, transforming the passions of fashion into territorial struggles, competition and violence.

The fabrication of scarcity

The energies of flirting, of plasmatic motility in the coupling of sensorial organs does not flow equally in all directions, and not all bodies are culturally entitled to feel desired or answer to the desires of another, and thus experience synchronized organ sensations. This is not only a matter of "forbidden love," depicted in classics such as in Romeo and Juliet, but cultures and social stratifications play part in the processes of embodiment and training of the sensorium, such as in taste (Bourdieu 1984) and the unequal aesthetic "distribution of the sensible" (Rancière 2004). Different social classes access the sensorial realm differently, and society provides certain form of sensual cultivation, while others are considered low or foreign. Similarly, access to prosthetics and training to use them in one's favor is also unequally distributed. The sensibility to read material compositions, color matching, silhouettes or cultural references is favored within certain groups, much like opera and classical art. Similarly, the cultivation of bodies, in swimming and ballet, or graceful walking in heels, designates certain behaviors and how plasmatic energies move throughout stratified bodies and society. The vectors and channels for processing fashion energy play an important part of this stratification; in pricing, sizes, cuts, proportions, etc. That is, while the process of fashionallaxis may on a basic level be open for almost anybody, its modulation and articulation is highly contested, competitive and entangled in the power-grid.

The stratification of fashion takes place through various forms of *fabrication*, the process of demarcation, delimitation, and materialization of affects. Fabrication in the realm of fashion means the production of scarcity, through *the control of fashion's vectors of realization*. Funneling the energies of fashion through commodities makes people associate fashion and flirting with brands, logos, shops, media, celebrities, while these are marginal phenomena in the biosocial pulsation of living energies. The fabrication of fashion limits the venues for flirtation, but also makes the consumers dependent on the goods for their self-esteem. If a consumer doesn't keep up with the materializations of the trends, he or she may lose self-confidence and feel unattractive.[48]

As noted by cultural critic McKenzie Wark (2004), power in

the cultural industries is dependent on controlling the vectors of realization, extracting value from the creativity of others. This happens in a similar way to the capitalist extraction of value from the industrial workers by controlling the means of production. For fashion however, this means the industry exerts control over the everyday *means of flirting*. And not unlike the values of supply and demand in the realm of commodities, the industry is dependent on the fabrication of scarcity. Like drug dealers, fabricators need addicts.

The fabrication of scarcity aligns with cultural processes enacted on an embodied and social level, in relationships between unequal agents. Price, sizing, or locations sort who can wear what, and the industry also controls the dissemination of expressions and styles. Another example is how copyright laws and courts today act as the upholders of sumptuary laws, manifesting the alliance between state actors and the exclusive expressions of certain groups with status. This in turn amplifies the Machiavellian usages of fabrication, bolstering the importance of the power-grid. Those who are connected to power get the connections and goods, more deals and "likes" and "followers" and move up the social hierarchies. Similarly, there is always a struggle over the domination of vectors, making them continuously migrate between centers, platforms and technological dynamics, accelerating the shift of styles, popular brands and expressions – also including the popularity of not "being fashionable" (Hollander 1978) or using vintage or DIY aesthetics. The upcoming brands try to usurp the current order, while simultaneously be acceptable enough to bring along followers and investors, accessible while still exclusive, different enough to be attractive, and affordable while still making sure the goods are in limited supply ("limited editions"). Today, even in the times of aesthetic and subcultural plenty, the distinction between "in" and "out" is still upheld.

Thus the functioning of fashion under its vectorial regime is always stuck in a mode of scarcity, turning the process of fashion into a *zero-sum game – for every person "in" someone else has to be "out."* This is the tragedy of fabricated fashion. While exclusion may be a basic form of a social dynamics, fashion comes to signify a mode of aestheticized relationships that promotes competition and envy.[49] With the fabrication of scarcity, the Umwelt of fashion is transformed from affirmation and an abundance of biosocial couplings into rivalries, fuelling anxieties of exclusion and possible humiliation. Such exclusive

Umwelts of fashion limit what a "body can do," turning unlimited possibilities into constrained and controlled bodies, hampering expressions and plasmatic motility, even as the environment seems free and participants can choose to wear whatever style they wish. I may be free to wear whatever I feel like, there are few sumptuary laws left in most Western societies (even if there are zoning and copyright laws with similar impact), yet if I want access to the nightclub I must internalize the tastes of this Umwelt, because I do not want to be rejected and be look like a loser. I learn what works and what doesn't work, and thus start to modulate or inhibit my desires and expressiveness to align with the winning formulas. I start self-regulating in an oppressive way, even as no person or institution has explicitly made me do so (for example, with threat of punishment).[50] As cultural critic Byung-Chul Han (2015) posits, under the regime of market-led freedom, everyone becomes an entrepreneur of the self, continuously promoting one's identity brand on the attention market, and forcing oneself to become auto-exploitative. With the continuous pressure to achieve and perform, the subject itself becomes a "project" under incessant development. Or as sociologist Zygmunt Bauman phrases it,

> "In the society of consumers, no one can become a subject without first turning into a commodity, and no one can keep his or her subjectness secure without perpetually resuscitating, resurrecting and replenishing the capacities expected and required of a sellable commodity." (Bauman 2007: 12)

Real Fashion; intersecting desire, anxiety and fear

The consumerist position in society is a key component for understanding the fabrication of fashion in contemporary society. Few people today are explicitly forced or repressed in the manner common in the time of Freud or Reich. Today's workings are much more subtle, and as pointed out by Han (2017). Populations are not primarily oppressed and exploited from the big Father or the State, but through the "free competition" of the fragmented social market place and attention economy, where *I am nothing if I do not do things*, "the I is now subjugating itself to internal limitations and self-constraints, which are taking the form of compulsive achievement and optimization." (2017:

1) In the absence of the big repressive "no" of Victorian times, and the orders of what one "should" do, today the imperative of freedom offers the promises of all that is possible, the "yes we can,"

> "Being free means being free from constraint. But now freedom itself, which is supposed to be the opposite of constraint, is producing coercion. Psychic maladies such as depression and burnout express a profound crisis of freedom. They represent pathological signs that freedom is now switching over into manifold forms of compulsion." (Han 2017: 2)

Instead of the negativity of the repressive state, the imperative to achieve fosters a continuous escalation of productivity, performance and self-exploitation, while setting atomized individuals to compete against each other in a race towards the bottom.[51] As Han notices, the dynamic of achievement society is a "totalized state of normality" in the sense of a "state of positivity" (2015: 48). Negativity is abolished, as it reduces performance, and people are instead coached to evermore affirmation. This is the new tyranny of continuously being required to become oneself, sell oneself, produce oneself, more and more.

The fabrication of scarcity in fashion places a key role in the intensification of these processes. Fashion does not repress or forbid as much as tempt and lure its prey deeper and deeper into addiction. Fashion is a promise of advancement on the attention market; "be different!" – "become yourself!" – "be an individual!" By highlighting the contrast to the beautiful celebrities, consumers are continuously held in a state of dissatisfaction and offered avenues to improve themselves, to be themselves more, to enhance their competitive edge on the attention market. But the celebrities do not order you, or repress you; they are your "friend." Some may be "influencers" and others may be "followers," but the promise is that there is no longer any master and slave. As Han posits, we are now in a society of perpetual work,

> "in which the master himself has become a laboring slave. In this society of compulsion, everyone carries a work camp inside. The labor camp is defined by the fact that one is simultaneously prisoner and guard, victim and perpetuator. One exploits oneself. It means that exploitation is possible even without domination." (Han 2015: 19)

Thus fashion is no longer a playful arena trying to escape the limits of the socio-economic domain as Lipovetsky (1994) would argue, but rather, fashion is at the core of the imperative of incessant aesthetic achievements. Fuelled with cheap and accessible clothes, making sure everyone is "able" to join in and start competing for a *position* within the attention economy, fashion has become an arena of tooth-and-claw, where it's all-against-all.[52]

To unpack the fabrication of scarcity in the realm of fashion, a perspective inspired by political realism can be helpful. Under the realist paradigm, relations between peers are always competitive and antagonistic. It is rivalry, not higher ideologies or deep drives, that trigger individual as well as collective behavior. Under scarcity, fashion is a zero-sum game in a limited number or arenas and available positions, with the quest for power taking shape in prestige and popularity. Indeed, under these conditions, it may be the very essence of fashion to be "nasty, brutish, and short" in a true Hobbesian way. Not only does realism move away from how things *ought* to be towards how they *are*, but dress is an explicit instrument for peer domination by processes of selection and rejection. Or in conjunction with Han's perspective, fashion offers the competitive edge over ones peers to perform oneself more and better, to achieve a higher "score" on the attention game.[53]

Thus, rather than merely a tool for seduction, under scarcity fashion is as much a weapon for rivalry, competition and aesthetic violence. And allure is as much seduction as deceit, and a lure a way to attract and ensnare prey. The peacock may still be beautiful and seductive, but it is also forcefully protecting its territory from antagonists and rivals. Pushed by socio-economic forces and fabricated scarcity, allure is a game of attraction, but also an aggressively seductive labor of prestige, deception, entrapment and predation.

Situating today's fashion in the "achievement society" of compulsive freedom and self-exploitation, does not disqualify Reich's ideas of societal repression, but frames other forces for the *concealment* of social process into character armor. Forced positivity and affirmation does not abolish fear and anxiety. It operates not so much under the dictatorial Father or State as much as in the fear of rejection, defeat, exclusion, discontent and negativity. In today's world, the worst thing that can happen is to be a "loser" – the ultimate disqualification of achievement.[54] When everyone should strive to "be himself or herself," yet the avenues for such endeavor are controlled by vectorial forces and fabricated scarcity (ex. fashion brands, or position on lists of influencers), to be an "individual" still means to conform with the rules of what counts as performance, achievement and success. Examining these circumstances may put a new light on the anxious armoring of the everyday fashion consumer and why conformity of dress still rules amongst the general population.

In the Umwelt dominated by the implicit characteristics of achievement, it is not explicitly the vectors which control the desires and anxieties of fashion. Places where the energies of fashion take center stage (ex. "fashion capitals") are not more dictatorial than others and social norms are loose and flexible. Yet, the pressure to achieve aesthetically may be even more intense in such places. In the competitive environment plasmatic motility is held back in self-regulation within individual bodies, and these seemingly free bodies come to deny and even fear the energies of their living plasma. Such process, even if emerging out of compulsive freedom rather than repression, still resonate with Reich's fear of plasmatic streamings (humiliation, fear, shame, pain) deep in the body, beyond the control of our rational mind. I may rationally think I do not compare myself to my peers, or that I imitate my idols, yet my non-conscious decisions still echoes throughout my Umwelt.

The very purpose of a Realist perspective on fashion, or what perhaps could be called "Real fashion", is to see how a certain type of social violence occurs in fashion, and may indeed be amplified by the current "fast" dissemination of cheap and accessible fashion. Not only is this violence veiled under the "shallowness" of fashion ("come on, it is only clothes"), it is also hidden under ideologies of individualism ("this is *my style*") and meritocracy ("because I'm worth it"), and thus fuses with these central contemporary values in Han's achievement society. From a perspective of political realism, the fashion industry funnels the emotions of flirting through commodities making it a zero-sum game: the quality of exclusivity comes at the price of exclusion. For every fashionable individual there is one unfashionable, to be "in" requires someone else to be "out," or as political theorist Carl Schmitt would have it, for every "friend" there is an "enemy" (Schmitt 1996). As Schmitt notices, "the political is the most intense and extreme antagonism" (1996: 29), and could the same be said about fashion as it is played out in the social arena? To Schmitt, the "friend and enemy concepts are to be understood in their concrete and existential sense, not as metaphors or symbols" (1996: 27), and could we also understand "in" and "out" not as symbolic demarcations, but as spatial and social categories (if you are "in" the bouncer lets you into the VIP lounge). From such perspective, a homology between fashion and a realist tradition of international politics seems possible. Supermodel Heidi Klum's famous line in the reality television show Project Runway, "In fashion, you are either in, or you're out," is thus more than a metaphor; it is the living emotion of antagonism the fashion industry strives to fabricate. It's like in *Top Gun*; all the heroes are young and beautiful, and they all know there are no points for second place.

Classic political realism, for example the work of Machiavelli, Thomas Hobbes or Hans Morgenthau, is based on the idea that Man, or the political human being, is an *animus dominandi*, that an inherent will to power makes Man inclined to dominate his fellows.[55] Hobbes' "state of nature," where life is "solitary, poor, nasty, brutish, and short" resonates well with Karl Lagerfeld's notion that fashion is "ephemeral, dangerous and unfair" (Lagerfeld 2007). This Realist Man (and perhaps "Fashionable Man") is not altruistic, peaceful, or rational, but as legitimate individual egotists compete about limited resources, Man becomes an *animus dominandi* (Morgenthau 1946: 164). Reich, however, would argue this hunger for destruction is only a secondary trait, stemming from the character armor and congealed through social processes, not something inherent to living functioning. This in some ways aligns Reich with a neo-realist or structural realist perspective on social relations, where the "nature" or "drives" of the human are irrelevant as it is not the nature of Man which affects politics, but the nature of insecure relations which produce the condition of *bellum omnium contra omnes*. As John Herz phrases it,

> [w]hether man is "by nature" peaceful and cooperative, or aggressive or domineering, is not the question. The condition that concerns us here is not an anthropological or biological, but a social one. It is his uncertainty and anxiety as to his neighbor's intentions that places man in this basic dilemma, and makes the "homo homini lupus" a primary fact of the social life of man. (Herz 1951: 3)

Mearsheimer's brute mathematics of the total war puts it more bluntly: "After all, for every neck, there are two hands to choke it." (Mearsheimer

2001: 31) From a realist perspective, fashion is "red in tooth and claw" and might is not only right; it is also beautiful. From a realist perspective, fashion is part of Machiavellian games of merciless aesthetic rivalry, employing allure as well as deceit to produce *adoration*, which is one of the most powerful tools of domination, making obedience and enslavement an experience of pleasure. The social congealment of this dynamic still produces subjective character-traits that adore charismatic and beautiful leaders.[56]

If, as fashion designer Karl Lagerfeld argues, fashion is "ephemeral, dangerous and unfair", Schmitt would add that *fashion needs to be so*, as both politics and fashion share demarcation and antagonism as their foundational principles. The political world is *by definition* a world of friends and enemies, us and them, in and out, of existential confrontation, and thus ruled by the law of the strongest and *most violent*, that is, the one achieving the best at the price of his or her rivals.

Armoring and the desire to be led

The competitive striving for aesthetic achievements under a regime of scarcity puts pressure on every relationship intensifying realist dynamics, turning participants into both auto-exploitative and self-repressive *collaborateurs* of fabrication. On a level of social relationships, dynamics of pride, envy, and rivalry come to shape the couplings between peers, affecting bodies and sensorial organs; each participant primed towards making it under dog-eat-dog dynamics.[57] Rather than a replacement of the repression in Reich's time, it is a dissemination and intensification of repression. To put it in another way; the "democratization" of fashion becomes a "democratization" of repression. Thus the process of congealment, which encrusts living functioning into armor, does not disappear, but is formed by peer-to-peer and relational factors, rather than by an oppressive State ideology.

Following Reich, the pain-induced repression of life energy petrifies the body and builds muscular armor that constrains the healthy flow of energy in the body. The organism becomes stiff and anxious and comes to fear life and freedom, resulting in subjects prone to feel a sense of exclusion, a desire to bully, to hate. As Reich (1973:

474) puts it, this is "the basic characteristic of *the murder of unarmored life by the human armored animal*," a key process of the societal phenomenon Reich calls the "emotional plague." Fashion is not any different: as looks and what is considered "acceptable" are socially regulated within a group, community, or subculture, the subject is socialized to the tastes of the group and becomes fearful of rejection and exclusion. Minuscule interpersonal signals regulate the looks between peers: a nod of approval or expressed interest reveals a successful advancement, while a side-look, frown, or marked silence may signify rejection.[58] The insecure subject becomes uncertain and tense: he or she can dress in any way possible, yet the fear of rejection turns into *a desire to be led,* and the subject asks to be designed and gives up his or her aesthetic agency to instead dress as a copy of one's idols.[59] This in turn reaffirms the aesthetic elitism that the fashion industrial complex thrives on; the "fashion supremacy" (von Busch 2014) where the elite of the rich and beautiful is inherently worth more than the poor and ugly.[60] Not unlike how the superior morality is always the morality of the superior, so the superior fashion is the fashion of the superior.

Reich's empirical theory of armoring offers a framework for capturing the biosocial anchoring of fear and anxiety into the body, in the fear of pain and plasmatic contraction. The process of armoring takes place in the character of the individual, but is affixed deep in the nervous system and muscles of the organism, or the muscular armoring. To Reich, these inhibitions are not situated only in a repressive superego or in subconscious distortions, but become embodied throughout the body, as *"instinctual desires and defensive functions of the ego, closely interwoven, permeate the whole psychic structure,"* and as Reich highlights, the psychic apparatus is not psychological, but *biological."* (1970: 116) Thus the armoring of the psychosomatic apparatus becomes layered, with a "stratification of the armor" (or *Panzerschichtung*), which like geological or archeological strata solidifies the historical experiences of the psychosomatic apparatus (1970: 121).

The armoring may give some stability and shape to the experiences and expressions of the individual (we may all need some of it to handle a bad day).[61] Armoring compromises the living functioning of the body as it resists plasmatic motility and organ sensation. For example, a deep moralistic and judgmental character is anchored in a restrictive muscular armor (1970: 156), and with prejudice and judgments the individual disengages with his or her sensibility. Escaping behind a comment such as "I am not interested," or "it's not my thing," are common ways to refuse to engage with emotional coupling, while simultaneously aching of curiosity. Thus armoring makes the person irrationally irresponsible as "the armor *restricts* the patient, his ability to be honest is part of his illness, and not malicious intention" as one may come to think (1970: 144). In anxiety, or remotion, the organism retreats towards its center, petrifying its motility. "Anxiety is to be understood fundamentally as a central stasis of fluid," thus the armoring effects all the inner plasmatic functions, causing an overall shrinking of the organism (Reich 1982: 47). The patients discomfort at feeling the plasmatic motility of the living core makes him or her feel comfortable in the armor and desire it to be there, indeed the patient is *fearful of the armor disrupting.* (Reich 1970: 204f)

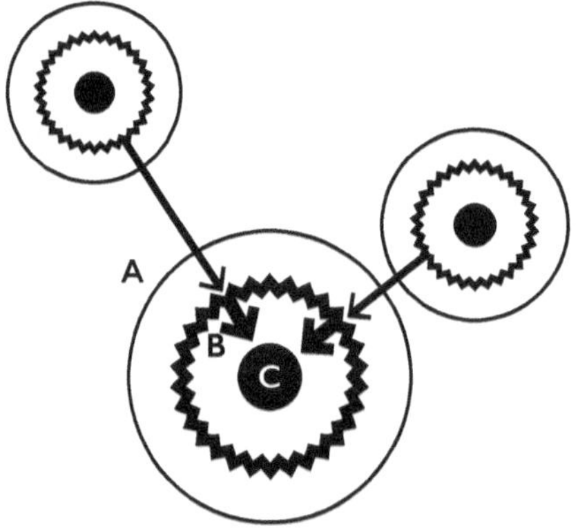

The structure of the armored individual is layered in, A; the periphery or mask, B: the (unconscious) armoring, C; the living core of the organism. Armoring emerges as an answer to social repression, but also from the judgments and rivalries between peers where armoring processes add to each other

Reich maps three layers in the armored and "cultured human," and this map is worthy citing at length,

"On the surface he carries the artificial mask of self-control, of compulsive, insincere politeness and of artificial sociality. With this layer, he covers up the second one, the Freudian 'unconscious', in which sadism, greediness, lasciviousness, envy, perversions of all kinds, etc., are kept in check, without however, having the least lost any of their power. This second layer is the artifact of a sex-negating culture; consciously, it is mostly experienced only as a gaping inner emptiness. Behind it, in the depths, live and work a *natural* sociality and sexuality, *spontaneous* enjoyment of work, *capacity for love*. This third and deepest layer, representing the *biological nucleus* of human structure, is unconscious and dreaded." (Reich 1970: 204)

It is the armoring dynamic between these layers that amplifies the anxiety and fear within the individual which makes a person potentially an "irrationally reacting mass of protoplasm" (Reich 1970: 205)[62] The tensions may become unbearable for the individual, who seeks to relieve his responsibility for "the *economy, individual and social, of the biological energy*," that is, he wants to set the energy at work, but release himself from the responsibility.

> "Passing this responsibility enthusiastically from himself to some Fuhrer or politician has become one of his essential characteristics, since he is no longer able to understand either himself or his institutions, of which he is only afraid. Fundamentally, he is helpless, incapable of freedom, and craving for authority, for he cannot react spontaneously; he is armored and expects commands, for he is full of contradictions and cannot rely on himself." (Reich 1970: 205)

This in turn leads to a desiring of being led where people exchange their potentialities for individual freedom for *illusionary* freedom, that is freedom through identification with an idea" (Reich 1970: 208) It is thus the fearful armoring which makes "*the masses of people themselves asserted to their own subjugation*" as people crave authority more strongly than they wish for independence, even when they are seemingly rebelling.[63]

The fear of freedom also highlights that fashion, as enacted through the industrially fabricated scarcity, becomes a form of *vital violence*, we have to deal with what Reich calls the "sex-economic" actions in the socius or social body, through which social and psychic repression enhance each other with violent or even deadly consequences. This is also where the Reichian questions of the conflict between the longing for life and freedom, and the *fear of life and freedom*, come to surface. Here, fashion, the wonderful pleasure of aesthetics, is perverted to come intimately connected to rejection, exclusion, bullying and violence.[64]

Paraphrasing the central question of Reich's work on the mass psychology of fascism; in 1933, *how could the German masses be made to desire their own repression?* We have to ask a realist question for fashion; *how do people come to desire to be subjugated under the aesthetic elitism of fashion, how do they develop a desire to be led, to have someone else legislate life and looks?* How does the processes of fabrication make people fear their freedom to dress in any way they feel like? How is fashion, in some sense like fascism, "the expression of a tragic conflict in the human masses, the *conflict between longing for freedom and actual fear of freedom?*" (Reich 1970: 207) Following Reich, Deleuze and Guattari argue the masses are not "fooled" or "mystified" by fascism or hegemonic ideology, as they slightly rephrase the question: "Why do men fight *for* their servitude as stubbornly as though it were their salvation?" (Deleuze & Guattari 1983: 28)[65]

So the central question is: Can there be similarities between how the Germans in 1933 *desired fascism*, and how we today, under the regime of aesthetic achievements, come to *desire fashion*, in a time of seeming freedom and with unlimited and "democratized" consumerism? With its imaginal elements, fashion ties into experiences of increased pride and honor, and the continuous "eternal return" of styles keep referencing historical deeds, reminding us of past greatness and subcultural edginess; punks, mods, hippes, etc. Fused with aspirations of aesthetic grandeur and heroism on the one hand, and the explicit rejection of those considered unworthy, dirty, corrupt and "other," the ties between fascism and fashion are not only metaphorical. Of course fascism and fashion are very different, not least in the intensity of violence, but they seem to share overlapping value-systems, with an explicit elitism, devotion, unity, racism, and ableism. And they both loathe the weak, poor, old, ugly and other, when they are not used as exotic affirmations of elitist virtue by being mercifully embraced. As historian Roger Griffin (2007) points out, another common trait of fascism is the dream of *palingenesis*, rebirth, and such element may further propel the analogy beyond etymologic or metaphoric interest. As Reich also points out, there is a draw towards such mysticism in the masses desire for subjugation (1946: 68ff).[66] Whereas notions such as "fatherland," "surging of blood," and "racial purity," drew many defeated Germans towards the promises of glorious rebirth through Nazism, it is not far fetched to see similar mystical assurances echoing in the advertising for beauty products and fashion. Not only is the consumer going to be reborn into a higher personal manifestation, but as the narcissist L'Oreal slogan goes, it is "because I'm worth it" (and implicitly that means others are not). With each new fashion I am reborn, reincarnated into a higher form; more pure, more perfect. And only I am truly worth it.

Following Reich, we should not search for an answer in ideology, in state power, or that fashion is merely a capitalist "illusion", but the answer lies in the human body and in the biosocial dynamics of a multitude of aesthetically desiring bodies. Bodies that all collude and collaborate with power, trading a "lesser suppression" of being a "slave to fashion" for the narcissist pleasure of subjugating others, making sure these targets of exclusion become the true victims of fashion. We must ask; is there potential violence residing in the vital affects of fashion, hidden under veils of "shallowness?" Or to put it another way; perhaps fashion is so socially powerful *exactly because it is considered shallow*, where competitors are free to attack each other's self-esteem, social standing and vulnerable souls, to seek the glory that can only be fully experienced in the triumph over a defeated rival, the vanity that is best produced in contrast against the "other". Is there a vital desire for violence promoted through fashion, as much as seduction and allure?

The violent functioning of force

In the realm of everyday dress, we can see how armored functionings may affect aesthetic rivalries, and manifest themselves in prejudice and cruel judgments, but also in social practices such as gossiping, exclusion, humiliation, bullying, shaming, and other forms of aesthetic abuse. The gossip media thrives in paparazzi exposure of celebrities where its very pleasure is to humiliate idols, and usually with their choice of clothes as an excuse. As the famous couturier Charles Frederick Worth remarked already in 1895, "Women dress, of course, for two reasons: for the pleasure of making themselves smart, and for the still greater joy of snuffing out the others." (Worth cited in Poland & Tredre 2009:9). This same continuum may go all the way to direct violence and ultimately actual killing because of dress rivalries. Such behavior may be seen as social deviances from how fashion ought to be, or that such aesthetic violence is not only occurring in fashion, but also in other forms of social distinction. But it is exactly by being considered "shallow" fashion becomes a socially acceptable arena for exclusion and violence, which otherwise would be condemned, and the triviality of fashion disguises exclusion and domination as popularity and seduction. To take an everyday example, it is illegal to discriminate between who can or cannot access a restaurant because of race, but considered perfectly fine for the bouncer to refuse entry to colored guests because "no sneakers tonight." Similarly, the in-crowd mark their territory in the school cafeteria by uttering "*nice* shoes" in a snarky tone, while everyone present knows it means "don't come and sit with us." And the so-called democratization of cheap and accessible fashion spreads the dynamic from the elite to the farthest corners of the market. The more accessible the aesthetic weapons become, the higher the stakes of the arms race: if I can afford to look good (as my peers), should I not care more about my appearance?

In Deleuze and Guattari's use of Reich, they emphasis how the mind, conscious and unconscious, belongs to the realm of physics and interoperating material and biological functions between the world and self, what they call "machines." There are no essentialist instincts or drives, such as *Eros* or *Thanatos*, but desire is the outcome of couplings and assemblages between various material and biological processes: schizophrenia is thus the normal condition of the mind. In correspondence with Reich's plasmatic functionings, the vitalism of Deleuze and Guattari's is not mystical but biological and physical, and they use "the term *Libido* to designate the specific energy of desiring machines" which in turn makes sexuality cosmic rather than reduced to "the pitiful little familialist secret."(Deleuze & Guattari 1983: 291f) The key point, highly relevant to the study of fashion, is that desire itself can never be deceived.

> "Interests can be deceived, unrecognized, or betrayed, but not desire. Whence Reich's cry: no, the masses were not deceived, they desired fascism, and that is what has to be explained. It happens that one desires against one's own interests: capitalism profits from this, but so does

socialism, the party, and the party leadership." (Deleuze & Guattari 1983: 257)

The sociopolitical coupling between sexuality and society, or psychological and social repression is also no metaphor, but a material one, where desires and love takes on sociopolitical form.[67]

> "The truth is that sexuality is everywhere: the way a bureaucrat fondles his records, a judge administers justice, a businessman causes money to circulate; the way the bourgeoisie fucks the proletariat; and so on. And there is no need to resort to metaphors, any more than for the libido to go by way of metamorphoses. Hitler got the fascists sexually aroused. Flags, nations, armies, banks get a lot of people aroused." (Deleuze & Guattari 1983: 293)

Thinking that fashion also is a realm of socio-political arousal is not far fetched. Fashion mixes aesthetic elitism with a special sense of meritocracy where the popular become entitled to their superiority, as in the ad-slogan *because I'm worth it.* A true fashionista gets aroused by his or her own aesthetic powers, as the good looks entail admiration, adoration and domination of his or her peers. The icons we see in media are all intricately bound to brands and designers, and not least our peer rivals. Thus the submission to fashion also pays off, and a fashion brand or celebrity makes for a strong authority or ally, however frail and ephemeral the bonds of loyalty may be. The fashion industry is the friend and armorer of every heroic warrior. Yet, where Reich sees fascism as a consequence of the repression of desire; negative, irrational, and a "lack" of released sexuality, Deleuze and Guattari (1983: 346) see fascism as its own desiring-machine, not a lack; an affirmative yet deadly war-machine where "desire desires its own repression."

Thus, if fashion is a living force in tune with our desires, it may also be corrupted, hijacked and turned against others and itself under competitive social dynamics.[68] And as noted earlier, if we extend biological selection mechanisms to the realm of dress, fashion is an extension of the evolutionary phenotype, struggling for territory. If beauty is, as Coco Chanel famously proclaimed, a "weapon," and looks indeed can "kill," the question becomes how this aesthetic power is utilized for popularity, admiration and power, and at what social cost.[69]

We should not naively think the energy of fashion is always personally liberating, but if captured in certain dynamics it can at any moment turn into to coercion, a threat or force. It is a passion that can possess its user. In Simone Weil's famous analysis of Homer's epic poem *Iliad* (Weil 2005), she notes that the main protagonists of the poem are not persons, they are mere puppets in the hands of the story's main hero: the holy rage, *thymos*, the force that makes things of men. In Weil's study, she traces the heroism, the intoxication to kill in the *Iliad*, to the warrior's dependence on the force. As Weil proposes,

> "The true hero, the true subject, the center of the Iliad is force. Force employed by man, force that enslaves man, force before which man's flesh shrinks away. In this work, at all times, the human spirit is shown as modified by its relations with force, as swept away, blinded, by the very force it imagined it could handle, as deformed by the weight of the force it submits to." (Weil 2005: 3)

To Weil, humans, by their very presence, have a violent influence on other human beings, turning enemies into things. However, those who are reduced to things do not have this ability: their fear has made them non-persons. The *Iliad* is full of this force, the force that kills:

> "How much more surprising in its effects is the other force, the force that does *not* kill, i.e. that does not kill just yet. It will surely kill, it will possibly kill, or perhaps merely hangs, poised and ready, over the head of the creature it *can* kill, at any moment, which is to say at every moment. In whatever aspect, its effect is the same: it turns man into a stone. From its first property (the ability to turn a human being into a thing by the simple method of killing him) flows another, quite prodigious too in its own way, the ability to turn a human being into a thing while he is still alive. He is alive; he has a soul; and yet – he is a thing." (Weil 2005: 5, original emphases)

As Weil notices, it is force that produces these consequences, both victors and vanquished, beasts and things, are transformed by force of rage. And this force is a living energy, propelling certain protagonists to heroic deeds or conquering and the humiliation of defeated foes. The heroes are possessed by force, and neither friend nor enemy can control it, but it is also an energy that corrupts through its success, through its vanity.[70] Is fashion also such force, an energy that possesses those who are fashionable, turning their seduction and flirting also into greed and envy, aggression and sadism, into forces beyond their control?

To German philosopher Peter Sloterdijk the *thymos* of Achilles is a force of vanity as much as hate, and it blazes from the impulsive center of the proud self. (Sloterdijk 2010: 11) This is a central observation; thymos is as much violent rage as it is a desire for glory, vanity, *amour propre*, ambition, and hunger for recognition. Vanity is not fair; it is deadly. The hero and his rage are indivisible, just like to Homer, "war and happiness are inseparable." (2010: 4) The virtue of the hero allows him to become a mediator or a "vessel for the abrupt flow of energy from the gods", and "just as the prophet is a medium in the name of the holy word of protest, the warrior becomes the tool for the force, which gathers in him abruptly in order to break through the world of appearances." (2010: 8) Heroism happens at the intersection between life and death, where an inner fear of living is turned towards the goal of conquering death to reach immortality, as cultural historian Ernest Becker (1973) famously points out. Becker in turn, with explicit inspiration from Reich, traces this quest to conquer death through excessive life to the very basic biological functionings of living organisms;

> "The protoplasm itself harbors its own, nurtures itself against the world, against invasions of its integrity. It seems to enjoy its own pulsations, expanding into the world and ingesting pieces of it. If you took a blind and dumb organism and gave it self-consciousness and a name, if you made it stand out of nature and know consciously that it was unique, then you would have narcissism. In man, physiochehemical identity and the sense of power and activity have become conscious." (Becker 1973: 2f)

As Becker argues, the same inherent striving for life in basic organism is translated into the human realm through culture and social arrangements, producing a narcissist heroism in denial of death, as,

> "man is not just a blind glob of idling protoplasm, but a creature with a name who lives in a world of symbols and dreams and not merely matter. His sense of self-worth is constituted symbolically, his cherished narcissism feeds on symbols, on an abstract idea of his own worth, an idea composed of sounds, words, and images, in the air, in the mind, on paper. And this means that man's natural yearning for organismic activity, the pleasures of incorporation and expansion, can be fed limitlessly in the domain of symbols and so into immortality." (Becker 1973: 3)

It is the hero, willingly submitting to the authority of the gods, who, by his or her heroic deeds, leaves time entirely to become culturally immortal. Fashion, in its continuous rebirth and becoming, may also be such a quest for undying greatness, as it denies aging, sickness and death in its celebration of youth, beauty and health. Yet, compared to the heroism of the legends, the deeds fabricated within celebrity culture may of course be trivial. Indeed, one can hardly argue style icons with armies of stylists and mountains of money are courageous in their choice of clothes, as if the public judgment would be harsher than the everyday harassments of an average teen in the institutional hell of the school corridors.

This is indeed the paradox of fashion in the lives of the heroes of fashion, that by becoming its ephemeral slave, they become timeless icons. Just think of the average celebrity on the red carpet and their many "collaborations" with stylists, designers and upmarket brands. Meanwhile, the countless teen grunts at the frontiers of inclusion and exclusion, putting their social lives at risk, are left to arm themselves with what their parents can afford them, yet they still live in the illusion that they are the creators of their own "style." It is indeed ironic that in the teens, the years most important to the formation of identity apart from one's parents, one is most dependent on the family's socio-economic status. As teens think of themselves as independent and setting themselves apart from their parents, they are often totally at the mercy of their family income, and this will probably mark their aesthetic sense of self and self-esteem for the rest of their lives.

So it may be of no wonder the mass market cheap and "fast" fashion is such a staple for youth, where most know what brands they identify with or not. These brands are the allies and authorities to shield the wearer from many peer struggles, if they are commercial brands, ethnic, street, or subcultural styles, through which one can seek belonging. But this centripetal process also shapes the domestication of fashion as an energy, making all too many fearful of dressing apart, of "coming out" as unconventional, different in the wrong way, or a potential target for peer judgment and rejection. Reich traces authoritarian submissiveness of individuals to the suppression of infantile and adolescent sexuality, as a process of submission just like "the castration of stallions and bulls serves that of securing willing beasts of burden." (1970: 195) But repression is also captured in culture and "civilization,"

> "Sex murders, criminal abortions, sexual agony of adolescents, killing of vital forces in children, perversions galore, pornography and the vice squad, exploitation of human longing for love by greedy and vulgar business enterprises and advertising [...] all these things could hardly be considered as ornaments of civilization." (1970: 199)

To these ornaments of civilization we could add industrial fashion and the willing submission to the fabrication of scarcity. Under such settings, the industrial fabrication of fashion is per definition unsustainable, and social life "nasty, brutish and short." The purpose of the industry is still to continuously undermine the self-esteem of its consumers, making them addicted to new goods, and in need of the industry to help fabricate a sense of self.

The fabrication of scarcity and rivalry, with the promotion of narcissist pride, greed, and envy, makes the fashion industry much like the arms industry, thriving in a setting of perpetual civil war, providing cheap arms to fearful combatants. As the force of flirting is processed through such social dynamics a realist game of power may easily take over the pleasures of plasmatic movement, cultivating more armoring even though it seems like "anything goes" in the market of style. More and more identities are offered at the expanding market, yet the basic fear of exclusion still drives the rivalry and consumers willingly give up their freedom and ask to be led with the hope it will give them a competitive edge against their aesthetic antagonists. Or even further, as Reich points out, they *desire to be led*, held captive by their fear of becoming losers, and thus willingly give away their freedom even without the explicit threat of force.

More cheap and accessible clothes will not alter this dynamic. Neither will sustainability in the sense of buying more emotionally durable pieces, or inheriting and repairing garments in a circular fashion. In consuming scarce goods, however ethical they are, the elitism, prejudice, judgments and armoring is left untouched. Also today, as young consumers spend more on experiences, athletics and well being, the dynamics of exclusion move along with the elite crowd. As Reich would argue, it is not the accessibility of pleasure that can challenge the armoring, but *"only the liberation of the natural capacity for love in human beings can master their sadistic destructiveness."* (1970: 197) Indeed, *"the human longing for life and pleasure cannot be banished"* Reich argues, *"but the social regulation of sexual life can be changed."* (1970: 191) A longing for flirting and connection through fashion is not going away, but we may rethink the way designers understand and operate with the living functioning of fashion in order to avoid funneling fashion through the fabrication of branded scarcity and the power-grid of positional goods.

The question designers should address is not "what will be the new exclusive look?" but, "what functions of plasmatic motility can we cultivate?" or to put it differently, "how do we support an abundance of flirting and desire?" With such questions, Reich's perspective on energetic functioning may help us think anew on the future of sustainable fashion.

FASHION FROM THE WELLSPRINGS OF LIFE

As Reich argues, repressed desire easily turns into desire for repression, and in contemporary settings of compulsive positivity, as Han suggests, the repression of the State or big Father is displaced into rivalries or performance and aesthetics to become enacted between peers. Thus most contemporary types of fashion are grafted into the liberal competitive economy to fuel positional competition and "ecologies of fear" where fashion is driven by fearful desires, or "liquid fear" as Zygmunt Bauman (2006) would have it.[71] Under this paradigm, fashion is funneled though the vectors and power-grid of fabrication, and the fashion industry, media, and education keeps reproducing this model, even under the label of "sustainability." Indeed, most approaches to sustainability in fashion never asks what is really to be sustained in the first place, instead an anti-social model keeps reproducing itself, but now draped in eco-cotton.

Seeing fashion as an energy of flirting has a potential of sidestepping some of the essential unsustainable elements in fashion, especially the issues of scarcity and the dependence on material waste in the process of fabrication. A biosocial perspective on fashion, seeing the energies of flirting as a sex-economy, could open new approaches to the practice of fashion design, but only if it finds ways to embrace an abundance of processes and practices. In such abundance, fashion could become a matter of individual as much as social health; a special streaming of life-affirmation echoing between peers as pleasure which possibly knows no boundaries. As the energy of flirting shines outwards, it can radiate onto *everyone* in the vicinity in an abundance of life. It is not something mystical, we can feel it when we enjoy time with a person radiating of life: their energy is contagious, we all feel more alive in their company. The most intense experience of fashion is like that: pure affirmation of life in togetherness. And this is at the essence of fashion as an experience: it is *an emotional rush one cannot experience alone.*

What designers have to approach is the question; how can the process of fashionallaxis become the object of design? Or rather; how can designers orchestrate the *abundance* of flirting and fashionallaxis, rather than the fabrication of scarcity? If we think of fashion as a *space we enter,* how can such space be more utopian?

Embracing a biosocial or orgone perspectives on fashion can open new vistas for practice but not least for fashion education. Seen from a larger perspective, environmental sustainability is perhaps the simple one to tackle, with agriculture, materials, dyes, washing, production, recycling and services, under an umbrella of "circular economics." What is missing is a radical questioning at the foundation of fashion: what is it really we want to sustain? How can we move beyond celebrity culture, following the "influencers" and asking to be led by designers in the first place? If fabrication is locked up in a mode of scarcity, fashion needs to find more generous ways to share the energy, attention and passions of flirting. A Reichian approach can help us with that. Taking inspiration from Reich we can think of fashion beyond commodities and into living functioning. Fashion can become a form of growth, exploration, training or therapy. Fashion could also be aimed at rehabilitating victims of rejection, anxiety, bullying and violence, building a healthier image of the body, but also self-knowledge and confidence.

This would require new kinds of being-with-fashion, a rethinking of fashionallaxis and the Umwelt constructed though fashion practice. As a point of departure, we could imagine ways of connecting fashion practice to what Reich calls the "wellsprings of life," which *thrive in abundance rather than scarcity.* These are *love, work and knowledge.*[72]

Fashion from the wellspring of *love*:

If we start with the matter of self-love and self-esteem, fashion has along way to go as the current model is based on undermining our sense of self worth and natural beauty. Not only must we develop ways of being a fashion designer that challenge the emergence of bodily disorders like anorexia or bulimia, but could we also imagine a type of fashion practice that collaborated with the health sector, working in tandem with body-focused therapies? How would such practice be designed, where a patient sees a therapist one week and a designer the next, remaking clothes for a new developing self? Could fashion be disassociated from the idea of turning oneself into a likable package, ready to be discovered on the markets of affection, and into more of an "art of loving," echoing Erich Fromm's (1957) famous argument.

The commodities of fashion have been a way to make designers move from the individual customer to more generalized trends and ideas of who their customers are (it is not very common for a designer to meet their average customers if working in the offices of the big brands). The many forms of social relations of fashion could thus also be opened though a lens of love. Not unlike how there is a plurality in the forms, expressions and intensities of love we can imagine many more forms of fashion; erotic forms (*Eros*), or more communal forms (*Agape*), or of siblings (*Philia*), or more instinctual affection (*Storge*), or even towards charity (for example in loving-kindness).

Could we thus imagine more loving relationships with special attention to the emotional journeys of love? On this more social note, could you have a weekly appointment with a fashion therapist like you would see a relational therapist? What would such a social event look like, where people come together with designers to cultivate a new sense of flirting? Would it be a form of self-development, couples therapy, or dating? Or if taken a more systematic approach, how would such biosocial therapy work?

What if designers think of fashion as *intimacy*? What way could designers open emotional and sensorial closeness to their users? What forms of intimacy with materials, processes and others can designers curate?

If we think of love as special form of attention?[73] Can fashion designers help cultivate attention to life, detail, presence, or even the more spiritual aspects of fashion; the process of self-transformation and the journeys of shape-shifting? If that loving attention is supported, we can imagine how fashion can be a training of the senses and a special care for seeing the other person, as a "who," and not merely "what" they are or wear. With attention towards the other we may also re-imagine the way we interact with clothes, not least in repairs: "I see your button is loose on your cardigan, let me help you attach it!" Here we can think of love as expansion, the joy of togetherness and shared growth and affirmation. This could be a joy measured in how my fashion-abilities help grow our shared experiences of happiness, not on how much cool stuff I have in my wardrobe.

Fashion from the wellspring of *work*:

Another field to address is the relationship to work and production that does not fabricate new forms of exploitation and scarcity. Today's fabrication of fashion is based on alienated labor, and the outsourcing of production not only to sweatshops overseas, but also to studios, interns and other forms of precarious labor. Few consumers can sew themselves and many pay to *not* have to engage with working on their clothes (or do the laundry). Thus the very understanding of work and care in relation to fashion has to be redefined.

We could for example imagine the work of fashion as a form of craft, for example as in Richard Sennett's (2008: 21) notion of craft where "people are anchored in tangible reality, and they can take pride in their work." For such crafts, would it be participatory events and workshops where people come together to work on their clothes as much as on their flirting? How would such training sessions be like?

Work is also about proximity to the materiality of the world and the body. It brings the world closer, into reach, imbuing the subject with sense of agency as the tangible world is within reach. Fashion is thus not an abstract or symbolic phenomenon happening "out there" but a force sticking to our bodies, orienting and aligning us towards each other.[74] Could designers help cultivate such proximities between work and our peers? Could "fashion hacking" and redesign of clothes be part of fashion addiction recovery programs? How is such an Umwelt curated, and how would the very notions of participation and co-design shift the way we perceive the *space of fashion*?

How would we think of fashion if we were to set parallel to the cultural schooling of the soul, like theatre, opera or art? On could fashion designers be employed by the public sector as co-producers, or curators of civic events; what public virtues would they contribute to? Using Reich's (1946) ideas of a "work-democracy," which he saw as the *natural* organization of work, emerging from the fostering of self-rule, self-governance, and sexual "self-regulation."[75] Thinking of fashion production under work-democracy could not least help us unpack how fashion could be produced through self-governed labor without exploitation, but also start imagining what sort of communities and utopian social ties fashion could help actualize.

Fashion from the wellspring of *knowledge*:

If self-knowledge and self-love were part if the points above, we must also speculate of the future of fashion knowledge and experimentation. A big part of fashion is the exploratory journey of becoming more than one thought of oneself, to discover new vistas of self and togetherness. If happiness is a sense of growth and expansion, how does knowledge help us grow as persons? What sort of knowledge do we need to cultivate that makes us connect and grow together with others, not in the sense of becoming a know-it-all, but the affirmative joys of creation and intellectual movement: of figuring things out.

On a very simple scale, crafts workshops and classes are part of such endeavors, learning new ways to be in the world, fixing things, understanding histories, relationships and techniques. The very journey of discovery brings joy, and even more when matched with a sense of homesteading, of building a place of one's own.

But we must also see knowledge as a form of deschooling (Illich 1971), or perhaps even an explicit unlearning of fashion-as-we-know-it, that is, deprogramming the competitive achievement focus which the paradigm of fabrication has turned fashion into. Indeed, a major problem with fashion education as well as consumption today is how its current form saturates so many arenas of society. The success of fashion, that it is all over media, makes too many of us think we know what fashion is, and thus we come to lack imagination of how it could be different. It is as if the current system is utopian, it just needs to be slightly more sustainable. Thus, as fashion is sustained in its current form, so its mechanisms of domination and servitude, anxiety and fear, remain unchallenged.

If we imagine fashion as a form of knowledge the settings of dissemination and exchange also changes; clothing libraries and archives can become sites of learning, and we can imagine economies of knowledge production; fashion labs and institutes where users deepen their engagement with self-knowledge. Residents and embedded participation can become part of the everyday operation in the processes of learning. As a consumer I do not want goods as much as the experience of widening horizons and deeper understanding of what I am part of. Instead of stores consumers visit fashion research institutions, monasteries and ashrams? What new types of languaging and fashionallaxis could such environments help develop, what new organ sensations?

Over the last years we have seen a movement away from the ubiquitous fashion hype as the wardrobes are full and consumers shift towards experiences, spas, gyms and other practices of wellbeing. However, not only are these experiences dressed, and often follow the trends, but they are still fabricated to reproduce vectorial dynamics and stratifies what is counted as enough improvement of the self.[76] As Han would argue, individual fulfillment and self-discovery can become yet another competitive arena for achievement.

Coming back to the homology of fashion and music we see how sound waves and beats make people move in unison while they stay separate. Music as well as fashion can be used in marching tunes as much as in soothing lullabies. But music can also help us imagine waves of sustainable forms of togetherness, like the never-ending cycle of new songs, only polluting the airwaves and our attention, but not destroying the planet through environmental disasters. Perhaps loving forms of fashion can be like love songs. And there is a continuous need for new love songs. Each new generation needs their new love songs, and the repertoire is endless, just like the wide spectrum of anticipation, eroticism, intimacy and disappointments of love.[77]

Every new couple experiences the loneliness, longings, desires and heartbreaks to new tunes and beats, and fashion is also an essential part of that process. Fashion is the flirting at the heart of biological being, an art of the animal, sharing the pulsations and plasmatic motilities of the loving life. Along the development of Reich's (1970: 343) work he encountered how sexuality opened up towards the more encompassing topic of "the living" and the problem of biogenesis; "Psychology came to be *biophysics* and genuine, experimental natural science. Its center remains always the same: the enigma of love, to which we owe our being." The plenitude of love songs, like the superabundance of emotions flowing between anticipating mates, marks the relentless desires for connection aching in organic bodies. Echoing de Botton, fashion can become a crucial democratic science, cultivating mutual ways of attraction in ways that will serve the many rather than the few.

Reich famously argues, "love, work and knowledge are the wellsprings of our life. They should also govern it." We could similarly imagine fashion being driven by the same wellsprings. And with love you will *feel it.*

To sum it up: *Love, work and knowledge are the well-springs of fashion, as well as life. They should also govern it.*

It isn't that capitalism has a grip on our consciousness so much as on our unconscious. It shapes the limits of what we can imagine. It does so because it has enjoyed decades of unchallenged domination, blitzing our nervous systems with its intoxicants, paralysing thought.

Mark Fischer

Endnotes

1. The term "provotype" is coined by Danish interaction designer Preben Mogensen (1992). To Mogensen a provotype can be a radical and generative prototype threatening the short sighted "taken-for-grantedness" of the routine. Through habitual frameworks and courses of action, artifacts often disappear from our perception by the very nature of their everydayness. A design provocation can have the ability to break through to open new vistas of thought. Thus, as Mogensen's suggests, the designer, or system developer in his case, should take on the role of the benevolent provocateur. Merging roles of maker, facilitator, and provocateur, the design of the provotype should create "discrepancies in the concrete" (Mogensen 1992: 22). "The idea from prototyping", Mogensen argues, "is to provoke by actually trying out the situations in which these problems emerge: provoking through concrete experience." (Mogensen 1992: 10) However, as noted not least through the Heideggerian perspective on everyday tools, the act of estrangement and provocation may be needed to actually engage with the instruments of Being. Thus, the prototyping approach challenges the preconceptions and "blindness" of the participants in the design process and puts new alternatives on the table (Mogensen 1992: 15f). Reich not only continuously questioned the roots of the disciplines he encountered, but he also drew out new passages between them. Exactly by connecting distinctly different fields, offering radically new ways of moving across disciplines, Reich's provocative ideas still challenge the "blindness" of established paradigms today.

2. Baudrillard (1996: 180f) describes the "Logic of Father Christmas" as a shared social ritual through which children, parents and the advertising industry all get what they want, and it is worth citing at length,

   > "Those who pooh-pooh the ability of advertising and of the mass media in general to condition people have failed to grasp the peculiar logic upon which the media's efficacy reposes. For this is not a logic of propositions and proofs, but a logic of fables and of the willingness to go along with them. We do not believe in such fables, but we cleave to them nevertheless. Basically, the 'demonstration' of a product convinces no one, but it does serve to rationalize its purchase, which in any case either precedes or overwhelms all rational motives.

Without 'believing' in the product, therefore, *we believe in the advertising that tries to get us to believe in it*. We are for all the world like children in their attitude towards Father Christmas. Children hardly ever wonder whether Father Christmas exists or not, and they certainly never look upon getting presents as an effect of which that existence is the cause: rather, their belief in Father Christmas is a rationalizing confabulation designed to extend earliest infancy's miraculously gratifying relationship with the parents (and particularly with the mother) into a later stage of childhood. That miraculous relationship, though now in actuality past, is internalized in the form of a belief which is in effect an ideal extension of it. There is nothing artificial about the romance of Father Christmas, however, for it is based upon the shared interest that the two parties involved have in its preservation. Father Christmas himself is unimportant here, and the child only believes in him precisely because of that basic lack of significance. What children are actually consuming through this figure, fiction or cover story (which in a sense they continue to believe in even after they have ceased to do so) is the action of a magical parental solicitude and the care taken by the parents to continue colluding with their children's embrace of the fable. Christmas presents themselves serve merely to underwrite this compromise."

3. This social abstraction could be drawn from the influential ideas of Alison Lurie (1981), Roland Barthes (1983) or Pierre Bourdieu (1984) who primarily situates fashion into the social realm as status and sign systems. The perspective presented in this essay enriches these views with a biological grounding.

4. As fashion theorist Susan Kaiser (2013) argues, we are all forced to "appear" to others, placing us as objects of cognition, and part of this process is judgment of senses: look, smell, sound, touch etc. Following the work on social cognition by Susan Fiske (2011), human cognitive processes are always tainted by judgment: "is this person I encounter a friend or enemy?" Fiske's framework places our judgment of people along the axis of warmness/coldness (how close should we get) and competence/incompetence (where in the social hierarchy do I place them?), but the essential claim is that the act of cognition is fused with the object's placement in a social status "grid."

5. Reich (1967: 23) stresses how the drives and its environment shape the organism in biosocial interaction, and the biological depths of the organism is affected by social behaviors; "The child brings with it a certain amount of energy. The world gets hold of it and molds it. So you have sociology and biology, both, in one organism."

6. Reich was highly inspired by his teacher, Paul Kammerer's, *Allgemeine Biologie* (Stuttgart: Deutsche Verlags Anstalt, 1915) where Kammerer makes probable

a life energy, or "form-energy" which would not be super-physicalistic, even if not yet identifiable with physical energies. Yet this energy is not mysterious, like the "entelechy" of Aristotle and Driesch, "but rather a genuine, natural *'energy,'*" that in turn is form-giving and transformative. Reich comes to define his "energetic functionalism" as a third position between mechanism and vitalism. See more of the vitalism-mechanism debate and Reich's position in Strick (2015: 22ff and 350).

7. Heller (2012: 425) explains the muscular function in armoring more in detail,

> "Muscle tone is influenced not only by the nervous system, but also by the quality of the irrigation of the tissues by blood. In becoming rigid, the muscle tissues acquire a particular metabolic quality that will afterward influence the vegetative dynamics and the functioning of the sensorimotor system. It then becomes possible to conceptualize that the defense system which structures the ego is in connection with the systems that structure and inhibit the behavioral repertoire."

8. Myron Sharaf (1994: 22) recollects Reich in an exchange with a patient, where he told her "You have a mask," and the patient replied, "You have a mask, too, Dr. Reich," whereupon Reich countered, "Yes, but the mask hasn't *me*." Here Sharaf highlights the difference between the rigid character armor of a neurotic person versus the flexible armor of the healthy person, which can open up when the person so allows.

9. The question of desired submission has a long history, at least stretching back to Etienne de La Boetie's question concerning people's "voluntary servitude" in *The Politics of Obedience: The Discourse of Voluntary Servitude*, (1576).

10.   It may be easy to dismiss Reich for his repeated claim that it is above all parental prevention of child masturbation that fosters the obedience and anxiety that leads to fascism. However, one must take into account how humiliation, shame and social pain are one of the strongest psychic markers of social transgressions (cf. Eisenberger *et al* 2003). Thus sexual repression must not today be read as a historic reminiscence of Reich's argument, but rather how deep anxieties can creep through social wounds. Even if today's sexual morals are in many places different from that of Reich's time, the emotional pain and humiliation emerging around issues of sexual expectations and performance are still shaping peer behaviors. (cf. Orenstein 2016)

11. The central nervous system is usually called "autonomic" in Anglo-Saxon literature, whereas Reich primarily follows the Germanic tradition of using the term "vegetative."

12. The organism itself builds the muscular armor to avoid the anxious contraction or pleasure of expansion, as both such movements are involuntary and connected to the animal within. As Reich posits,

> "The vegetative nervous system is thus a contractile plasma system, a contractile organ running throughout the entire organism. It represents the 'amoeba in the multicellular organism.' This is the explanation and the basis of the uniformity of the total body function." (Reich 1982: 125)

13. It is important to notice that attention and emotion are *physical* and *functional* processes, not merely an "inner" or spiritual experience. Reich's functionalism is explicitly bridging the dicotomies of mind vs. body or spritual vs. material. Anchoring the expansion and contraction of the organism in plasma motility deepens the connection between psychological, social and biological phenomena. As Reich posits, "If I want something I stretch out … If I am afraid, I pull in … I go out in love, I withdraw in anxiety. Our withdrawal is anxiety. That's simple. It's the plasma motion which does it." (Reich 1967: 74)

14. Reich often returns to the connection between simple organisms and human functioning,

> "The living process in man is functionally the same as in the amoeba. Its main characteristic is *biological* pulsation, the alternation of *contraction* and *expansion*. This process can be observed in single-celled organisms in the rhythmical contractions of the vacuoles or the contractions and serpentine movements of the plasma. In metazoan, its most obvious manifestation is in the cardiovascular system, where the pulse beat is clear evidence of pulsation. Its manifestation in the organism as a whole varies according to the structure of the individual organs." (Reich 1973b: 154)

15. Loving couples show how imitation and love usually comes hand-in-hand, and soon turn inseparable, as philosopher Aaron Ben-Ze'ev (2000: 415) highlights,

> "The desire to be with the beloved often becomes a desire to fuse with the beloved and in a sense lose one's identity. Lovers begin to develop similar likes to those of their partners; for example, to enjoy music to which they were previously indifferent"

16. Cultural critic Mark Fisher (2014), highlights how music produces a special form of "hauntology;" the failure to realize the music's utopian promise and materialize a radically new world. Parallels can be drawn to the many types of counter-fashion throughout history where people don special clothing in times of social upheaval or subcultural resistance, dreams which later come to haunt this type of clothing with its unfulfilled promise.

17. Reich notices that the orgasm reflex must be applied beyond the narrow sexual realm,

> "The function of the orgasm reflex cannot be, as one could assume from the viewpoint of a 'purposiveness,' to accelerate the passage of the male semen into the female genital organs. The orgasm reflex is independent of semen discharge for we also find it in the embryo in a typical forward position and convulsion of the tail end; in the whipping, energetic forward-movement of the tail end of many insects, e.g., in wasps, bees, bumblebees; and also in the customary position of the tail end and hindlegs in the species of dogs, cats, and hoofed animals. (Reich 1951: 46)

18. In Reich's theory of sexuality (1970), the orgasm stands out as the fulfillment of a healthy adult sex life, but also where the full orgasm is not primarily seen from the propagation of the species, but from the health of the total psychosomatic organism. In the orgasm, both biological and psychological tensions are released, from the biological tension and charge, to the psychological build up of longing, anticipation, and the promise of pleasure and bliss.

19. Expansion and shrinking is easily translated into emotions of pride and shame. As a cause to these existential experiences, Jean-Paul Sartre argues how the *look* ties human Being together with others. As social animals, humans are heavily dependent on others in evaluating experiences, as the perception of others, or "being-seen-by-others" is an essential part of the relations that form human Being (Sartre 1966: 341). The essential experience of being-looked-at is the feeling of pride or shame before the eyes of another. For example, the experience of shame, of being revealed, unveiled as a form of harassment, touches on the very formation of my Being, the *cogito* of the self: I do not only *know* shame, I *am* the shame (Sartre 1966: 248f).

20. If fashion is infused by passion in the sense of "life," this vitalism could be read in relation to the phenomenological sense coming out of Heidegger and Husselr and the "French thought" in Merleau-Ponty, Derrida, Foucault and Deleuze as these theorists draw together the living experience at the intersection of "inner" and "outer" life, not least the entwining of life, imagination and political power (see also Lawlor 2006).

21. A energy-oriented approach to fashion design would mean highlighting flows and intensities, rather than finished material commodities, which in turn resonates with ecologist David W Orr's notion of design as "the shaping of flows of energy and matter for human purposes" (Orr cited in Capra 2003). As Orr's notion posits, designs are never finished, but are continuous processes interacting in dynamic systems. If fashion is primarily seen as various degrees of energetic intensities and as flow of matter energy, it shifts the focus on designers

and consumers as primarily meddling with produced goods and symbols to instead see how they interact with, bend, and modulate energy flows. In Reich's perspective, organisms are transmitting stations of life energy, modulating energy which passes through the living system. As Reich (1951: 17) posits,

> "Form, to orgonomic functional thinking, is *frozen* movement. We know from ample evidence that the act of superimposition is due to bio-energetic forces acting beyond control. The two orgonotic systems involved are DRIVEN to superimpose by a force which, under natural conditions, i.e., not restricted by outer hindrances, is beyond their control. It is *involuntary* bio-energetic action."

22. Reich (1973b: 6f) points towards how metaphors such as a beloved person having a "magnetic" attraction, or how we feel "electrified" with excitement, corresponds to the bioelectrical charge of the organism. There is an unknown "something" in this energetic charge – "but the something itself is not electricity." Thus, flirting as a biosocial energy connects to Reich's studies of sexual interaction and bioelectrical charge. For example, Reich notices,

> "The fact that sexual compatibility exists between certain men and certain women is very remarkable phenomenon which until now has remained completely unexplained and has merely been glorified in mystical terms." (Reich 1982: 6)

23. As Heller (2012: 206) notices, the struggle between neo-Reichians and the more conventional natural sciences around the concept of orgone energy is often obfuscated by an unwillingness to examine one's own position,

> "The use of a scientific term to designate a notion considered unscientific in academia did reveal itself to be lucrative in terms of clients, but it reinforced the rupture that developed between academia and Reichian therapies. Even Reich would probably have objected to a procedure that is manifestly a mystification. To justify this approach, the neo-Reichians discredited the chemistry of the chemists a an inanimate mechanic; on the other hand, their Reichian energy was presented as being full of vitality that generates the universe. Yet an inverse argument could be directed at these Reichians who reduce the chemical dynamics to something foolishly mechanical. They know so little about chemistry that they fail to grasp the unbelievable creativity that is activated thanks to chemical and atomic operations."

However, using orgone as merely a metaphor would strip the radical foundation of Reich's ideas. A great potential of the concept is not only scientific, but as Corrington (2003: 247) argues, it connects separate domains of knowledge,

> "What makes the orgone concept so interesting is that it straddles the divide between science and metaphysics. It emerged from Reich out of decades of

preparatory research, and he felt that the cumulative evidence for its existence was overwhelming. But some his claims about orgone went beyond the reach of his experimental protocols, and he extended the concept in highly meta-phorical and poetic ways. This does not mean that the extensions were inva-lid; rather, he entered in a different order of discourse, one less continuous with the science than he assumed."

While Corrington has a point, it is important to see orgone as something more than a metaphor or a conceptual tool to bring it closer to a scientific fact. A discrete way could be to think of orgone in relation to Jacques Der-rida's concept of "weak force," or Gianni Vattimo's "weak thought;" not pri-marily something that *is*, as ultimate objective truth, but instead it *calls*, as an opportunity for philosophical reconstruction. (Derrida 2005: xiv) A "weak orgone" could be thought of as emotional bioenergy or affect, perhaps in resonance with the works of neuroscientist Antonio Damasio. Or tie it's agency to matter-energy, as in Actor-Network-Theory where also matter acts on subjects, which in many ways would resonate with Reich's earlier works on bioelectricity. A strong perspective on orgone, on the other hand, would approach the energy as a scientific fact, as a motor energy, and it can charge organic matter, for example supported by Strick (2015). Drawing a continuum between "weak" and "strong" orgone would do some violence to the coherence of Reich's work, yet it allows a moment to embrace the weak promise of orgone as more than metaphor while still leaving the door open towards the strong part, and also resonates with the position taken by some of Reich's supporters, such as A.S. Neill and Ola Raknes. In this designerly interpretation of Reich's ideas, the emphasis is on what orgone can *call* us to think and do, yet fashion is "stronger" than affect. At the very least, thinking fashion as orgone energy (weak or strong) can make us *work differently*, and offers an *opportunity for radical reconstruction of fashion.*

24. Reich primarily discusses emotions and uses affect interchangeably, even if he also posits emotions influences others. In much of the more current literature, affect is a contagious diffusion of emotions, moving seamlessly between matter, minds and media (cf. Massumi 2002, Gregg & Seigworth 2010). However, as Ahmed (2015: 204ff) poignantly argues the focus on the diffusive phenome-non on affect risks forgetting the deep anchoring in the unity of the body, and instead giving affect the new privileged status that the mind had before, and also forgetting how feminist scholars for a long time have challenged the mind-body dualism (206).

> "Drawing on the etymology of the word, I became interested in emotions as how we are moved, as well as the implied relationship between movement and attachment, being moved *by* as a connection *to*. Following many other femi-

nist theorists, I am deeply concerned with how feeling in the body is moved: who could even think of feeling without also recalling physical impressions: the sweatiness of skin, the hair rising; or the sound of one's heartbeat getting louder?" (Ahmed 2015: 209)

Ahmed's work highlights how emotions "stick" to objects, bodies and signs, for example, how the "stranger danger" stick to the bodies of the other, or happiness sticks to objects of desire; "Certain things become good *because they point toward happiness.*" (Ahmed 2015: 219)

25. Tarde's notion of the "germ" is not unlike what Dawkins (1976) calls a "meme," a cognitive replicator, or a "virus of the mind" in Brodie (1996).

26. According to Reich, orgone energy is attracted to organic material, and these materials collect orgone from the cosmos, while metallic materials first attracts but then quickly repel or reflect orgone. Thus it is possible to accumulate orgone energy between organic and metallic layers, concentrating them within an "orgone accumulator" (not unlike a faraday cage). One must wonder if it is possible to charge or re-charge orgone energy into clothes through orgone accumulators.

27. It is important to notice that Reich also sees a wider application of the sexual energy than mere genital experience (1970: 29f). Rather, there is a whole spectrum of experiences and emotions, from the passions of the genital to wider social and cultural forms of excitation and striving for life. As he notices, for the teenager, after at least partially satisfying his hunger, starts looking for a girl friend,

> "If he has no girl friend, he wants personal independence and the means to find a girl and make her happy. Cinema, theatre, books, decent clothing, and a room for oneself are elementary desires of every human being from adolescence to middle age. The driving factor here is yearning for sexual happiness, both in the narrow, sensual sense and in the broadest cultural sense." (Reich 1976: 164)

28. Reich was himself surprised at his discovery of the energy emitted from the samples in his lab. As Reich mentions in his notes March 6th 1939,

> "Have just spoken on the phone with Dr. Bon in Amersfoort. *Because I am radiating* – at the hands, palms, and fingertips, at the penis. Bon said it could be very dangerous, 'not yet too late.' Marie Curie may have dies from it. I must not go to pieces. *But I'm radiating.*" (Reich 1994: 193)

Later, on March 28, Reich frames the energy more conceptually in his journal,

> "Orgone is a type of energy that is the opposite of electricity; it is the specific form of biological energy. In keeping with the orgasm theory, which equates

the sexual and vegetative [autonomic nervous system], it must at the same time be the specific sexual energy, orgasm energy." (Reich 1994: 199)

29. Flirting is can be seen as a sexual continuum from looks, talk, touch, all the way to sexual intercourse, but also on many scales, much in tune to Reich's idea of "orgonotic superimpositions" which can happen on cellular levels as well as on cosmic scales as a *transindividual* happening (Reich 1951: 18).

> "Reduced and abstracted in its purest form, superimposition in the biological realm appears as the approach through *attraction* and full bio-energetic *contact of two orgonotic* STREAMS. Membranes, organs, fluids, nerves, will-power, unconscious dynamics, etc, must be discounted here, since they do not constitute superimposition. Superimposition of two orgone streams appears as a common functioning principle (CFP) of nature which *fuses* two living organisms in a specific manner—specific to the *basic* natural function, and not to the two organisms. In other words, *superimposition of two orgone energy streams reaches, as a function, far beyond biology.*"

30. These are energies which do not exist in isolation, they act like magnetism, pulling together two or more components through mutual attraction. The energy of fashion is a potentiality enacted through mutual attractive forces, or to put it differently, fashion is an energy *amplified by mutual growth.*

31. In Reich's view, the armoring and "emotional plague" makes people fear and envy those with health orgone streamings. For Reich, this type of envy has nothing to do with status, or sexual envy of "conquests," but with the *quality of living functioning* a body can be capable of. It also unlocks also historical events, such as the murder of Christ (and people's desire for Barabbas),

> "Christ was killed in such a shabby way and he was defiled by a sick and sickening crowd because he dared to love his body and did not sin in the flesh. Christ was tortured because they had to destroy his truly godly, i.e., orgonotic way of life, strange and dangerous to them. They mocked him and laughed at him and threw ugly words at him because they could not suffer to be reminded of godly life within themselves." (Reich 1971: 153)

32. As Theweleit argues, masculine culture is fearful of the "weakness" of femininity and its fluid form; it is a fear of contamination. The feminine threatens to corrupt charachter and steadfastness (much like passion can corrupt and undermine reason.) Appearing weak is the first step to this downfall. Barbara Ehrenreich notices in the foreword to Theweleit (1987), fascism is commonplace in much male culture and fantasy,

> "As Theweleit says, the point of understanding fascism is not only 'because it might "return again",' but because it is already implicit in the daily relationships of men and women. Theweleit refuses to draw a line between the fantasies of

the Freikorpsmen and the psychic ramblings of the 'normal' man: and I think
here of the man who feels a 'normal' level of violence towards women (as in, 'I'd
like to fuck her to death') [...] Here Theweleit does not push, but he certainly
leaves open the path from the 'inhuman impulse' of fascism to the most banal
sexism." (Ehrenreich in Theweleit 1987: xv)

33. Becoming-animal must not be thought of according to anthropomorphic categories, but as a drift along a continuum of functions and couplings. For example, Deleuze and Guattari mentions how,

> "A racehorse is more different from a workhorse than a workhorse is from
> an ox. Von Uexkull, in defining animal worlds, looks for the active and pas-
> sive affects of which the animal is capable in the individuated assemblage of
> which it is a part. For example, the Tick, attracted by the light, hoists itself
> up to the tip of a branch; it is sensitive to the smell of mammals, and lets
> itself fall when one passes beneath the branch; it digs into its skin, at the
> least hairy place it can find. Just three affects; the rest of the time the tick
> sleeps, sometimes for years on end, indifferent to all that goes on in the
> immense forest. Its degree of power is indeed bounded by two limits: the
> optimal limit of the feast after which it dies, and the pessimal limit of the
> fast as it waits. It will be said that the tick's three affects assume generic and
> specific characteristics, organs and functions, legs and snout." (Deleuze &
> Guattari 1987: 257)

34. Biologist Humberto Maturana argues for a composition of living which resonates strongly with the functionalism of Reich, positioning Being as a cognitive
coupling between the singular organism and its environment;

> "Systems as composite entities have a dual existence, namely, they exist as sin-
> gularities that operate as simple unities in the domain in which they arise as
> totalities, and at the same time they exist as composite entities in the domain
> of the operation of their components" (Maturana 2002: 12).

This position is similar to that of biosemiotics, as Soren Brier (2008: 339) argues, biosemiotics is founded on "a bioconstructivism – that is, they see every
living system constructing its own 'life world'".

35. Reich's student Ola Raknes introduced exercises where the patient would
explore imagining being a jellyfish, and let movement and breathing move freely through the body. (Heller 2012: 545)

36. From Reich's (1951: 50) perspective of orgonotic functionalism, animal cop-
ulation is a coupling or superimposition of orgonotic streams,

> "The orgone, concentrated at the genital end and urging forward, cannot get
> out of the membrane; it is forced backward again acutely. *There is only ONE
> possibility of flowing out in the intended forward direction; BY FUSION WITH*

A SECOND ORGANISM. The direction of excitation of the second organism agrees with the direction of the orgone wave in the first."

Flirting could thus be seen as a two superimposed streamings of orgonotic attention, where push and pull work in conjunction, drawing two living systems into sync, entwining streamings, attracting each other towards sexual acme where the streams burst through the membranes of the self.

> "The genital embrace grows out naturally from a slowly developing total body urge to merge withe another body. One can easily see this basic characteristic in birds, toads, butterflies, snails, in mating deer and other freely living animals. The final delight of total energy discharge in the orgasm is the spontaneous result of a long continued build-up of smaller delights. These little delights have the faculty of providing happiness, yet creating desire for more. Not always do the smaller delights lead toward the final supreme delight. Two butterflies, male and female, may play with each other for hours and then separate again without embrace. They may go further and superimpose without penetration. [...] The total organismic excitation precedes the special genital excitation. The orgastic potency grows out of this total body delight and not from the genital." (Reich 1971: 29)

37. Flirting as a biological phenomenon could also be compared to evolutionary biologist Lynn Margulis' theories of "symbiogenesis," which refers to the origin of new forms of organisms by establishment of long-term or permanent symbiosis (Margulis 1998: 6). The symbiotic focus is a bright contrast to the vulgar Social Darwinist notion of the "survival of the fittest," where evolution is reduced to violent competition, to instead highlight evolution through close cooperation, exchange and merger of different species. This means that some species evolve in close symbiosis rather than rivalry. This concept similar to mutualism and explores special biologic niches where cooperation challenges competition as the driving force of evolution, as highlighted by popular physicist and ecologist Fritjof Capra (1996).

38. Drawing upon the ideas of French philosopher Georges Bataille's ideas of the "general economy" (1991), this energy of fashion is a matter of natural abundance, like the energy emanating from the unconquered sun. Bataille's sees economy as the act "in which the 'expenditure' (the 'consumption') of wealth, rather than production [is] the primary object" (1991: 9). Bataille's general economy considers living matter in general, and comparing with nature, this economy always produces an excess of life, an excess of energy that in turn adds pressure, like nature reclaiming an untended garden path in summer (1991:30). In a similar vein, fashion is an energy and squandering is the process through which it lives. Like love, it is based on continuous giving and will die if made

scarce. When transubstantiated and fabricated into products, garments and accessories, the goods are ritually sacrificed by the shifting seasons. This squandering metabolism of luxury is in Bataille's view the prime expenditure of social energy (together with war and religion).

39. It could be worth noting that both Galliano and Bissinger's examples place fashion commodities as the lure towards performing sex (sex as achievement), and not a process of allure and seduction. As Reich (1971: 26) notices,

> "The longing for the fusion with another organism in the genital embrace is just as strong in the armored organism as it is in the unarmored one. It will most of the time be even stronger, since the full satisfaction is blocked. Where Life simply loves, armored life 'fucks.' Where Life functions freely in its love relations as it does in everything else and lets its functions grow slowly from its beginnings to peaks of joyful accomplishment, no matter whether it is the growth of a plant from a tiny seedling to the blossoming and fruit-bearing stage, or the growth of a liberating thought system; so Life also lets its love relationships grow slowly from a first comprehensive glance to the fullest yielding during the quivering embrace. Life does not rush toward the embrace. [...] Armored man, on the other hand, confined in his organismic prison, rushes for the fuck."

40. Deleuze and Guattari (1983: 295f) suggests a limitless sexual revolution on the molecular scale where all parts have the possibility to amalgamate with the other, escaping molar, binary and State sexuality, and thus,

> "everywhere a microscopic transsexuality, resulting in the woman containing as many men as the man, and the man as many women, all capable of entering—men with women, women with men—into relations of production of desire that overturn the statistical order of the sexes. Making love is not just becoming as one, or even two, but becoming as a hundred thousand. Desiring-machines or the non-human sex: not one or even two sexes, but n sexes. Schizoanalysis is the variable analysis of the n sexes in a subject, beyond the anthropomorphic representation that society imposes on this subject, and with which it represents its own sexuality. The schizoanalytic slogan of the desiring-revolution will be first of all: to each its own sexes."

41. It could be noted that Reich himself was a man of great allure. As Peter, his son, posits; "He was larger than life. He radiated heat. Women looked at him the way men look at women." (Reich 2015: vii)

42. Maturana and Varela (1992: 75) argues,

> "Every ontogeny occurs within an environment; we, are observers, can describe both as having a particular structure such as diffusion, secretion, temperature. In describing autopoietic unity as having a particular structure,

it will become clear to us that the interactions (as long as they are recurrent) between unity and environment will consist of reciprocal perturbations. In these interactions, the structure of the environment only *triggers* structural changes in the autopoietic unities (it does not specify or direct them), and vice versa for the environment. The result will be a history of mutual congruent structural changes as long as the autopoietic unity and its containing environment do not disintegrate: there will be a *structural coupling*. [...] We speak of structural coupling whenever there is a history of recurrent interactions leading to the structural congruence between two (or more) systems."

43. Guattari (1977: 93) builds similar couplings, and plasmatic functionalism much in correspondence with Reich,

> "It is never a man who works—the same can be said for desire—but a combination of organs and machines. A man does not communicate with his fellow men: a transhuman chain of organs is formed and enters into conjunction with semiotic links and an intersection of material flows. It is because the productive forces of today cause the explosion of traditional human territorialities, that they are capable of liberating the atomic energy of desire."

44. Maturana and Varela (1992: 210) argues,

> "We operate in language when an observer sees that the objects of our linguistic distinctions are elements of our linguistic domain. Language is an ongoing process that only exists as languaging, not as isolated items of behavior."

45. Uexkull's Umwelt as a cognitive realm, echoes with Reich's concept of "organ sensation",

> "Nature inside and outside ourselves is accessible to our understanding only through sense impressions. Sense impressions are at bottom sensations. And the sensations are essentially *organ sensations,* or otherwise expressed: *We make contact with the surrounding world with organ movements (= plasmatic movements).* Our emotions are the answers to the impressions of the environment. In perception, even in self-perception, sense impression and emotion flow together into functional unity." (Reich 1949: 50)

Organ sensation is an "integral part of our ego sensation, and simultaneously a part of objective nature. In orgonotic functioning, we perceive our very selves." (Reich 1949: 51) Armored individuals, with their organs rigid, lose this unmediated connection to the world, and thus come to withdraw and live "in their heads." Today, Reich's ideas resonate well with much of the findings in embodied cognition.

46. Reich does not explicitly use Uexkull's terminology, but his biosocial perspective shows many commonalities with Uexkull's biology, not least Reich's notion of "organ sensation."

47. It is important to not overlook the power relations in both fashion and flirting; a flirt can be a stolen look/attention in the form of eyes diverted from another object in a limited attention economy. Similarly, fashion can be a stolen
look as a look/outfit needs to be multiplied and imitated to be fashion. In both
instances there is a dynamic of who-has-agency-over-another and could be
thought within frameworks of appropriation and preconceived cultural rights.

48. As Bauman (2010: 59) posits,

> "Time flows on, and the trick is to keep pace with the tide. If you do not wish
> to sink, keep surfing – and that means changing your wardrobe, your fur-
> nishings, your wallpapers, your look, your habits – in short, yourself – as
> smoothly as you can manage. [...] Armies are no longer made of conscripts;
> instead staying 'with' and 'in' fashion is now achieved by universal conscrip-
> tion, sanctioned with capital (in the sense of social death) punishment for
> desertion."

49. Rene Girard's (1965) perspective on "mimetic desire" would argue rivalry and
envy between peers is inescapable as the intensity of desire stands in relation to
the competition it propels. However, from the perspective of the industry, the
fabrication of scarcity increases these dynamics of desire and it is in the interest
of the fashion system to fuel this fire. Even if the fragmented fashion system of
today cannot uphold the strict demarcation between "in" and "out" as in the
time the decrees from Paris was the ruling word, this does not mean the distinction does not exist. Informal dress codes are still enforces at night clubs,
and ask any teen what brands and styles are the "right" ones at school and they
will draw clear lines on what counts and what does not.

50. The Reichian perspective offers a compelling framework for tracing the connection between organic grounding of biosocial functioning and the scale of
the compound sociopolitical practices of the masses. Or if applied to fashion,
from the desires of the individual to the aggregated super organism of fashion
as a viral meme, possessing the minds and bodies of its hosts. The energy of
fashion is the connection between the two levels, just like orgone is to Reich.
As Deleuze and Guattari (1983: 292) argues,

> "As to the whole of Reichian theory, it possesses the incompatible advantage
> of showing the double pole of the libido as a molecular formation on the sub-
> microscopic scale, and as an investment of the molar formation on the scale of
> social and organic aggregates."

51. It may seem Han's argument clashes with the primacy of repression in Reich's
analysis of the social order. But as Reich (1946: 23) explains, *"every social order
produces in the masses of its members that structure which it needs to achieve its
main aims,"* and this would resonate with how a neoliberal governmentality

utilizes fashion and aesthetic rivalry to amplify the entrepreneurship of the self, mobilizing all affects into relentless self-promotional labor, as in the examples of Berardi (2009) and Crary (2013). Guattari (1977: 94) argues in a similar manner where "we are witnessing other fascisizing micro-crystallizations, which succeed the phylum of the totalitarian machine." Here, we see a new stage of capitalism,

> "Unlike fascism, capitalist totalitarian machines endeavor to divide, particularize, an molecularize workers, meanwhile tapping their potentiality for desire. These machines infiltrate the ranks of the workers, their families, their couples, their childhood; they install themselves at the very heart of the workers' subjectivity and vision of the world." (Guattari (1977: 96)

52. This merger between neoliberal economics and democracy, or rather, how the everyday notion of democracy has become equivalent to the free market entrepreneurship of the self is also overlooked by Joshua Miller (2005) in his excellent text on fashion and democratic relationships. As Han (2015b) would argue, today democratic relationships have come to be synonymous with market relationships, not least in their encouragement of ubiquitous "openness" and "transparency," which does not offer deeper civic engagement but only a sense participation while agency and power moves towards those with capabilities to harvest data and attune public opinions.

53. Han's argument about the pressure to achieve resonates with Yohji Yamamoto's comment that as a fashion designer you do not exist if you do not make new collections; "our business it is very competitive. Because it's a rat race about the amount of business; and we have to win." (Yamamoto in Wenders 1989)

> Wim Wenders: "If you would stop for one season, what would happen? Would you still exist as a designer?"
>
> Yohji Yamamoto: "No. When you stop once then we would say, 'He's finished.' So, it means you can't stop."

54. The fascist personality evolves in the efforts of the family to make a "good" child; shy, obedient and afraid of authority, paralyzing rebellious forces and inhibiting thinking and critical faculties,

> "In brief, the goal of sexual repression is that of producing an individual who is adjusted to authoritarian order and who will submit to it in spite of all misery and degradation. At first, the child has to adjust to the structure of the authoritarian miniature state, the family; this makes it capable of later subordination to the general authoritarian system. *The formation of the authoritarian structure takes place through the anchoring of sexual inhibition and sexual anxiety.*" (Reich 1946: 25)

Following Han's inversion of the repressed subject into a "project," parallels can today be drawn to the production of high-achieving entrepreneurial "can-do" children, nervously preparing for Ivy-league already in kindergarten, which anchors the status anxiety of the family into the very being of the child.

55. Keeping the masculine notion of human being in this political definition of humankind puts focus on how this notion posits certain male-oriented values or cultural traits; machismo, virility, erectile potency – which overlaps well with Reich's male focus on the nature of the orgasm.

56. Reich blames the Marxists in pre-war Germany for not understanding the divergence between economic position and psychological mass structure, and thus failing to rally the masses as they kept repeating rational economic arguments in hope to win followers,

> "Vulgar Marxism schematically separates economic existence from social existence as a whole and contends that human 'ideology' and 'consciousness' are *immediately* and *exclusively* determined by the economic conditions. In doing so, it arrives at a mechanistic antithesis of economy and ideology, of 'base' and 'superstructure.' It considers ideology dependent, schematically and one-sidedly, on economic conditions, and overlooks the dependence of economic development of ideology. For this reason, the problem of the 'retroaction of the ideology on the economic base' remains inaccessible to vulgar Marxism." (Reich 1946: 10)

As Reich (1946: 15) posits, mass psychology must concern with the desires of the people and how these support irrational decisions, or make people reactionary to the ideology which supports their struggles,

> "In social psychology, the question is quite reverse: What is to be explained is not why the starving individual steals or why the exploited individual strikes, but why the majority of individuals do *not* strike. Socio-economics, then, can satisfactorily explain social phenomenon when human thinking and action serve a rational purpose, when they serve satisfaction of needs and directly express the economic situation. It fails, however, when human thinking and acting *contradict* the economic situation, when, in other words, they are *irrational*."

57. Reich also pointed towards how sexuality and love are not always used in virtuous ways, but can be weaponized. James Wyckoff explains in his biography on Reich (1973: 36),

> "Reich pointed out again and again that both sex and love are used as weapons, for pleasure at the expense of another person, for security, for power. It is always contempt for the living. In this sense, the difference between murder (whether of not it goes under the name of war or crime) and the dirty joke is negligible. Both are assassins, and the difference is only in degree."

58. As noted by Heller (2012: 426) it is important to notice how much of Reich's ideas on the sociopolitical production of muscular armoring and judgment, and the body's regulation of the psyche, overlaps with Pierre Bourdieu's ideas of taste, distinction and habitus.

59. In the character structure of the mass individual there occurs an *identification* with the authoritarian leader, where the individual becomes one with the movement, identifying with the strength of the leader. This tendency in Nazi Germany,

> "is the psychological basis of *national narcissism*, that is, of a self-confidence based on identification with the 'greatness of the nation.' The reactionary middle class individual believes he discovers *himself* in the Fuhrer, in the authoritarian state. On the basis of this identification, he feels himself the defender of 'the nation,' even though, on the basis of this very identification, he despises 'the masses' toward whom he has an individualistic attitude." (Reich 1946: 53)

60. Reich highlights how fascism is not a political alignment as much as a psychological disposition and desire of the individual steeped into mysticism,

> "Fascism is not a political party but a specific Weltanschauung and a specific attitude toward people, toward love and work." (Reich 1946: xix)

61. Heller (2012: 502) emphasizes Reich's ideas that the armor is to be controlled and not control the patient.

> "What the Reichian therapist then defends is the possibility of *oscillating* between openness to oneself and openness to another. This pulsation can have different timing. The oscillation can happen in a few seconds or a few months. The state of constriction is a closing off to self and others, like in certain extreme types of depression. Knowing how to pass from one state to the other is vital."

62. The three layers of the human character, the "core," the "middle layer," and the "periphery" gives a practical tool to trace the dynamics between biosocial pulsations and the armor,

> "Human beings live emotionally on the surface, with their surface appearance. [...] In order to get to the core where the natural, the normal, the healthy is, you have to get through the middle layer. And in that middle layer there is terror. There is severe terror. Not only that, there is murder there. All that Freud tried to subsume under the death instinct is in that middle layer. He thought it was biological. It wasn't. It is an artifact of culture. It is a structural malignancy of the human animal. Therefore, before you can get through to what Freud called Eros of what I call orgonotic streaming or plasmatic excitation (the basic plasma action of the bio-ener-

getic system), you have to go through hell. Just through hell!" (Reich 1967:
109)

63. It is important to notice that for Reich (1946: x), fascism merges anti-author-
itarian with authoritarian longings; "Fascism is not, as is generally believed, a
purely reactionary movement; rather, it is a mixture of *rebellious* emotions and
reactionary social ideas." Reich highlights how the rebelling German middle
classes were themselves stuck with a respect for authority;

> "This ambivalent attitude—*rebellion against authority with simultaneous respect
> and submission*—characterizes any middle class structure at the period of
> transition from adolescence to maturity and is accentuated by straitened cir-
> cumstances." (1946: 30f)

Today, we can draw parallels to similar types of rebellion in how youth use
slang, style and music to rebel and distance themselves from their family, to
express their independence. But with fashion, there also comes a willing submission to the new rules and leaders and a hunger for aesthetic authority.
While the distance from family authority may be widened, new authority
quickly fills the gap, that of keeping up with one's peers, something Reich
also posits in a passage about the use of clothing for the middle class individual;

> "He lives in straitened circumstances but keeps up appearances, often to a
> ridiculous degree. He feeds himself poorly but invests in 'decent clothing.' The
> silk hat and the Prince Albert coat became the material symbol of this charac-
> ter structure. Few things are, at first glance, more characteristic of a popula-
> tion than its clothing. The attitude of "Keeping up with the Joneses" specifi-
> cally distinguishes the middle class structure from that of the industrial
> worker." [with the added footnote, "In America, the middle-class character of
> the industrial workers obliterates this distinction." (Reich 1946: 40)

64. Guattari (1977: 88) builds on Reich and argues for an interaction between
State organization and individual desire, and that "there is a politics which ad-
dresses itself to the individual's desire, as well as to the desire which manifests
itself in the broadest social field. [...] The despotism which exists in conjugal
of family relationships arises from the same kind of libidinal disposition that
exists in the broadest social field." Furthermore, Guattari sees fascist desires
conjugate into *machinic composition,* much like chemical composition into a
"chemistry of desire," which promotes micro-fascism,

> "what fascism set in motion yesterday continues to proliferate in other forms,
> within the complex of contemporary social space. A whole totalitarian chem-
> istry manipulates the structures of state, political and union structures, insti-
> tutional and family structures, and even individual structures, inasmuch as

one can speak of a sort of fascism of the super-ego in situations of guilt and neurosis." (93)

It is however important to notice how Guattari also differs from Reich, not least in his rejection of Reich's view on sex-economy and ideology. As Deleuze (1977: 101) writes in a foreword to one of Guattari's essays,

> "We can see how this orientation differs from Reich's; there is not a libidinal economy that would subjectively prolong through other means political economy; there is not a sexual repression that would interiorize economic exploitation and political subjugation. Rather, for Guattari, desire as libido is already everywhere, sexuality surveys and espouses the whole social field, coinciding with the flows that pass underneath the objects."

65. Dagmar Herzog (2016: 18) examines Reich's influence on the works of Deleuze and Guattari, and highlights the need to reassess Reich's work,

> "In general, as Deleuze and Guattari's reappropriations also help us see, it has become all too easy in hindsight to make fun of Reich – and no doubt we are still influenced today both by Freud's repudiation of him during the desperate flight from Nazism (and the perception that Reich's Marxism was too toxic to be associated with) and by the stark naivety of some of the liberationist projects pursued in his name in and around 1968. What is lost from memory in the current smirkily complacent consensus, however, is not only the genuinely innovative insights Reich offered at the time into the sophisticated, and after all, stunningly effective emotional work done by Nazism. Also lost is the fact that quite a few of those insights were subsequently taken up, albeit without giving Reich credit, by the far more consistently celebrated although otherwise mutually opposed figures of Erich Fromm and Theodor Adorno"

66. As Reich posits in the *The Mass Psychology of Fascism* (Reich 1946: xvi), translated into English first after the war;

> "Today it has become absolutely clear that fascism is not the deed of a Hitler or Mussolini, but the expression of *the irrational structure of the mass individual.* Today it is clearer than ten years ago that the race theory is biological mysticism. Today, one is closer to an understanding of the orgastic longing as a mass phenomenon than ten years ago; there is more of a general inkling of the fact that *fascist mysticism is orgastic longing under the conditions of mystification and inhibition of natural sexuality.*"

67. As noted by Sara Ahmed (2015), it is important to not forget how fascism uses love to mobilize patriotic emotions and xenophobia: hate toward the other is not propagated in isolation, but in conjunction with the love of the nation and family. This resonated with Reich's (1946) observation, that it is *out of love*

that fascist violence has to be used to protect the mythical values of the "blood" or "nation."

68. As cultural theorist Gilles Lipovetsky notices, the contemporary rule of "total fashion" seeps into all our relationships, as "the consummate reign of fashion pacifies social conflict, but it deepens subjective and intersubjective conflict; it allows more individual freedom, but it generates greater malice in living." (1994: 241)

69. It is important to notice how also passions can "possess," thus making claims of ownership and appropriation, transgressing boundaries of who controls whom. The arrows of Amor are weapons and a passion is often a mix of pain and pleasure (and the orgasm a *petit mort*, "little death.") As noted by Jean-Luc Nancy and Adele can Reeth (2017), joy and *jouissance*, pleasure, can be understood as a form of property and consumption, of transgression and expropriation, but it also challenges these boundaries. As an ecstasy it signifies a situation of "being-outside-of-oneself",

"'Take me!' is not necessarily a neurotic demand: There is a sense of capture and possession, of belonging, which is beyond legalistic, dominating appropriation. In 'You belong to me,' 'I belong to you,' what does this 'to' mean? Is one being alienated? Devoted? Exposed?" (2017: 10)

70. One of Reich's followers, Ola Raknes, frames how Reich grounded his views on politics through the biological,

> "[Reich] showed how the natural longing for contact and happiness had been perverted into mutual dependence between the political leaders and their followers, how competition, distrust, and craving for power took the place of natural collaboration and mutual satisfaction." (Raknes 2004: 26)

71. As Bauman argues, our culture ravages in fear, "fear or being left behind. Fear of *exclusion*." (Bauman 2006: 18) Bauman ties the neoliberal notion of freedom as primarily enacted within a sanctioned spaces of picking between consumer goods, yet what we see in every popular media narrative is *"people trying to exclude other people to avoid being excluded by them"* (Bauman 2006: 19).

72. It must however be noticed that the sense of growth and abundance always has the possibility to corrupt, that the desire for production, expansion, reproduction (and achievement, as Han would have it), is always at risk of deducting with the lure of power, but also of setting the superior norm and increasing rivalry. This sense of growth is no mere figure of speech, but the biological grounding of emotion, thus the more dangerous.

> "It was not by means of metaphor, even a paternal metaphor, that Hitler was able to sexually arouse the fascists. It is not by means of a metaphor that a

banking or stock-market transaction, a claim, a coupon, a credit, is able to arouse people who are not necessary bankers. And what about the effect of money that grows, money that produces more money?" (Deleuze & Guattari 1983: 104)

As mentioned earlier by Reich, *love* can be a weapon, and so can of course *work* and *knowledge* (as Marx and Foucault would argue). Yet, building from these wellsprings would allow a grounding of practice in biosocial functioning. Then the task is to train, working outwards from there, aiming to avoid stasis, armoring, and fabrication of scarcity. Starting closer to the open source can keep the stream(ing) slightly clearer.

73. Reich (1949: 52) argued for love as analogous to attention,

> "*Orgone biophysics operates with organ sensation as a **first sense** of a strict physiological nature.* In order to investigate nature, we must *love*—using the word literally—the object of research. Expressed in the language of orgone physics, we must have immediate and undisturbed *orgonotic contact* with the object."

74. Ahmed (2015) presents a profound discussion on the "stickiness" of affect to bodies and how to engage and transform this phenomenon.

75. For an in-depth discussion to Reich's notion of work-democracy, see Philip Bennett (2010).

76. Even if designers would strive to help educate users to become fashion-able, rather than buying fashionable commodities, there is a normative risk in what this "ability" means to perform. If the ability is aimed at simply making the user able to "keep up" with the latest trends, little has been won. Like the notion of "wellness," ability can easily become a new guideline for stratification. The very notion of "ability" thus needs to be diversified and deepened to reflect richer nuances of Being and togetherness.

77. As Deleuze and Guattari (1983: 331) argues,

> "Psychoanalysis ought to be a song of life, or else be worth nothing at all. It ought, *practically*, to teach us to sing life. And see how the most defeated, sad song of death emanates from it: *eiapopeia*. From the start, and because of his stubborn dualism of the drives, Freud never stopped trying to limit the discovery of a subjective or vital essence of desire as libido. But when the dualism passed into a death instinct against Eros, this was no longer a simple limitation, it was a liquidation of the libido. Reich did not go wrong here, and was perhaps the only one to maintain that the product of analysis should be a free and joyous person, a carrier of the life flows, capable of carrying them all the way into the desert and decoding them"

In a similar vein, the task is never to "save" fashion from fabrication or armoring, and not even save it from itself, but to ask how fashion can be closer to the wellsprings of life, how fashion can be a joyous love song to life, a flirting with the cosmos never held back by anxiety and fear. Reich's endeavor echoes throughout this search.

Or paraphrasing Robert Smith, at its best, just like a love song, fashion can make me feel like I am free again, like I am clean again, like I am young again, like I am fun again.

Disclaimer: The artist recognizes that these experiments are his own, and that they do not in any way represent Reich's experimental work. Reich, for example, measured voltage changes at the skin surface in varying states of emotion-- *not* resistance, which these electrodermal measurements track. More fundamentally, Reich's understanding of the medical function of the orgone accumulator was not that it "charged" or "filled up" nonliving substance. Rather, he emphasized that the accumulator had an orgone energy field, and when an experimental animal or a human subject sat in an accumulator, a mutual excitation between the energy field of the organism and that of the accumulator resulted-- a non-mechanical process. Thus, the idea that items of clothing could be "charged" in any way that would influence a human being is the author's notion based on a very different idea, that contrasts sharply with Reich's experimentally-based findings about orgone energy.

LAB DOCUMENTATION

The lab-based research examining the energy of fashion in *Vital Vogue* is based on a series of designerly provotypes. As provotypes, the props are not made to prove ideas or enact research, and they are thus not meant to engage the scientific status of Reich's work, nor do they in any way represent Reich's experimental work. More than seeking proof of concept, they offer a glimpse into new possible Umwelts and magical environments for fashion: an opportunity for philosophical reconstruction of what fashion is, based on the energies of bodies.

The experiments have taken two directions. The first part concerns the bioenergetic charge of fashion in the body, measuring the electrodermal activity (EDA) of neurally mediated effects on sweat gland permeability. This activity traces the relationship between emotional arousal and sympathetic activity and is measuring the skin's electrical conductance, which varies with its moisture level. The tests resonate somewhat with Reich's (1982) research on the bioelectrical affects of arousal and anxiety and visualizes how basing fashion on energies can change our perspective.

The second part concerns the orgone charge of clothing, examining if fashion as an energy can charge the organic materials of clothing, turning garments into intensifiers of fashion. Perhaps garments recently active in flirting processes contain traces of energy, or could be recharged, becoming active again with bodies as orgonotic exciters? The important issue here is to see fashion as an energy, stronger than affect: it is not only a mimietic and intersubjective experience, but has impact *inflicted* on our bodies and emotional lives.

When we read the word fashion, the concept should connote *electricity*, not *garment* or *image*; think *power-grid*, not *fashion system*.

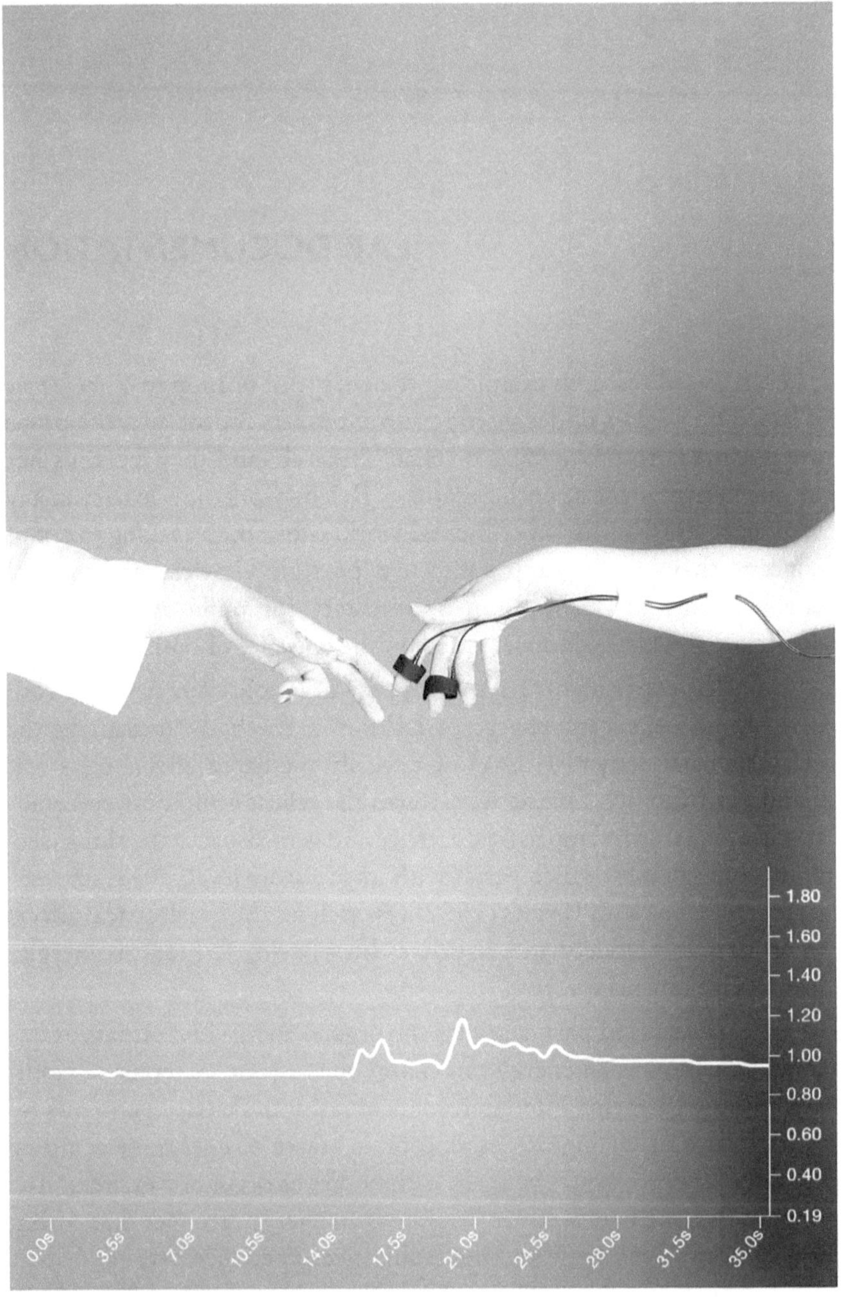

1.80
1.60
1.40
1.20
1.00
0.80
0.60
0.40
0.19
0.0s
3.5s
7.0s
10.5s
14.0s
17.5s
21.0s
24.5s
28.0s
31.5s
35.0s

2.00
1.50
1.00
0.50
0.24
0.0s
5.5s
11.0s
16.5s
22.0s
27.5s
33.0s
38.5s
44.0s
49.5s
55.0s

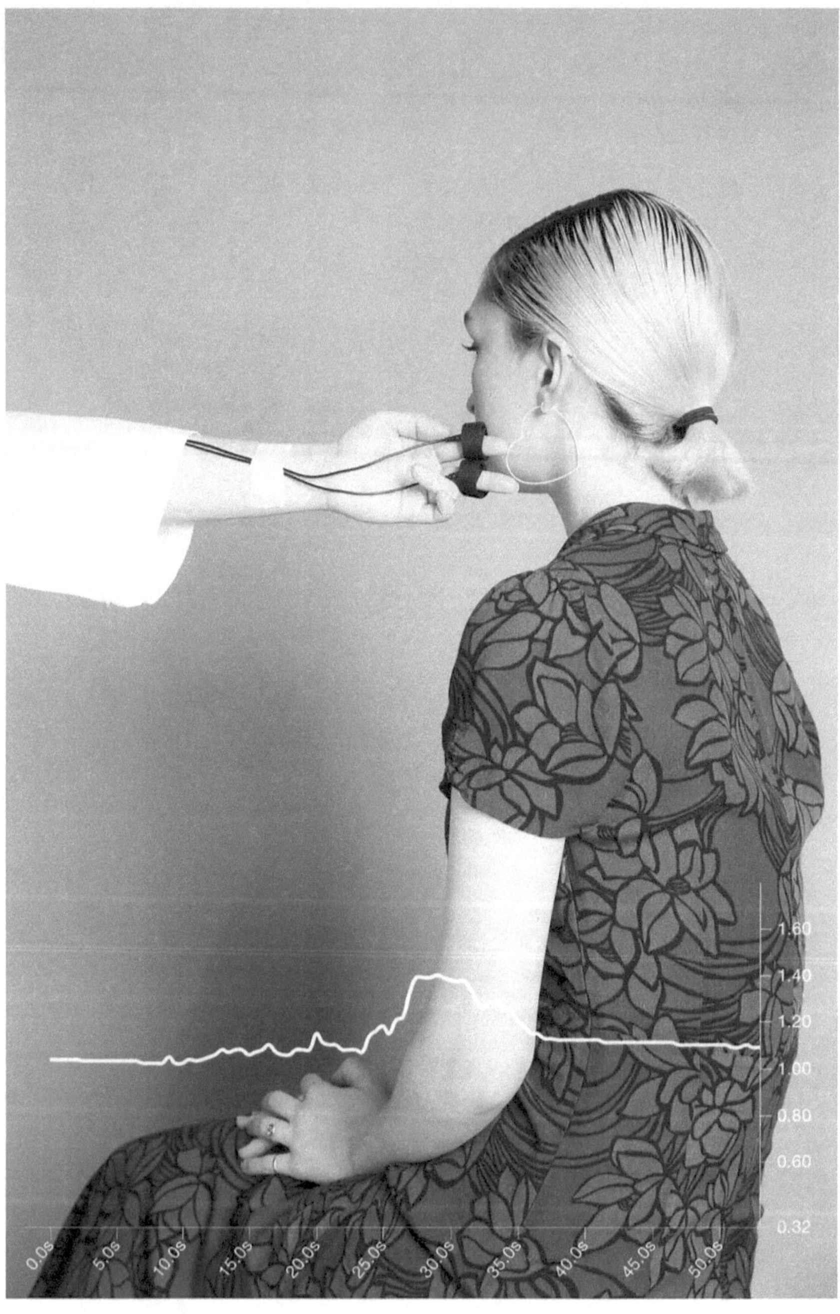

1.60
1.40
1.20
1.00
0.80
0.60
0.32
0.0s
5.0s
10.0s
15.0s
20.0s
25.0s
30.0s
35.0s
40.0s
45.0s
50.0s

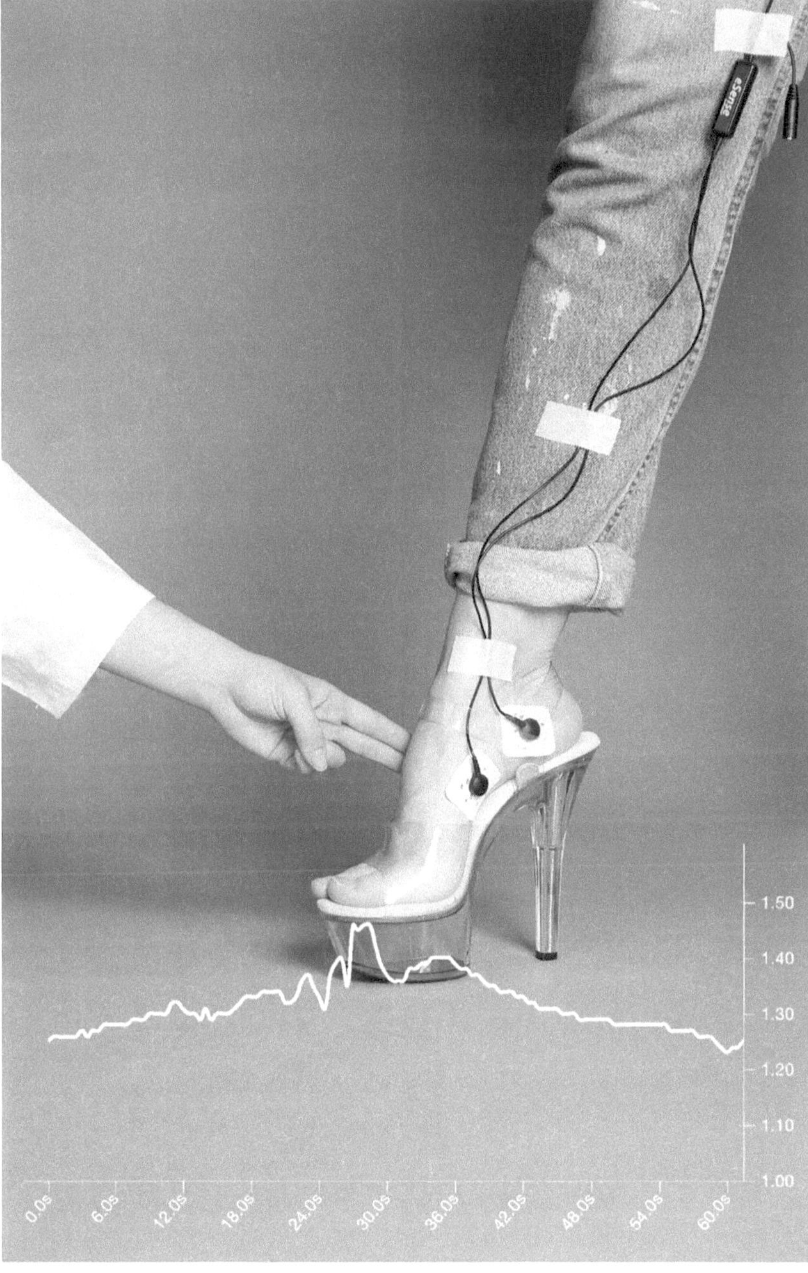
1.50
1.40
1.30
1.20
1.10
1.00
0.0s
6.0s
12.0s
18.0s
24.0s
30.0s
36.0s
42.0s
48.0s
54.0s
60.0s

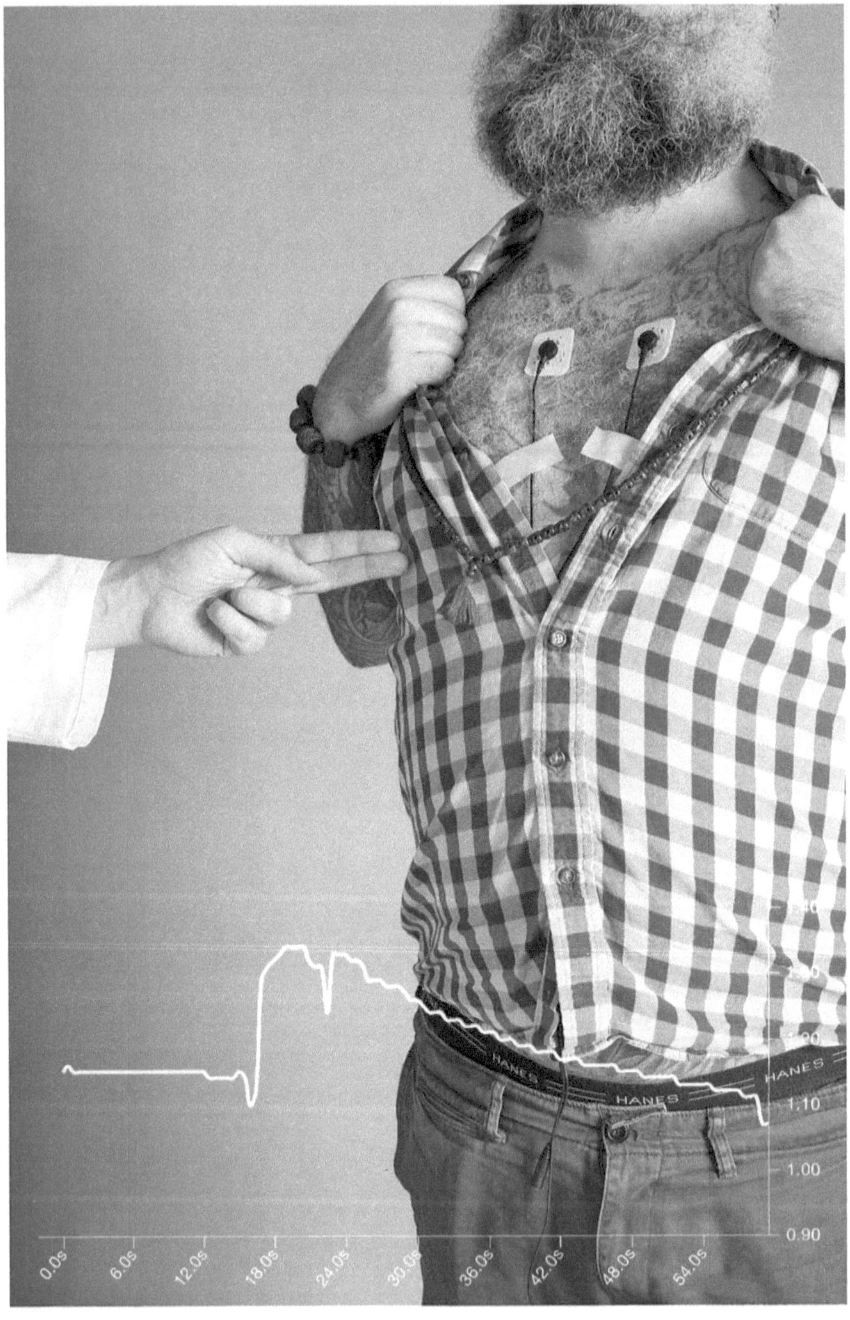

HANES
HANES
1.40
1.30
1.20
1.10
1.00
0.90
0.0s
6.0s
12.0s
18.0s
24.0s
30.0s
36.0s
42.0s
48.0s
54.0s

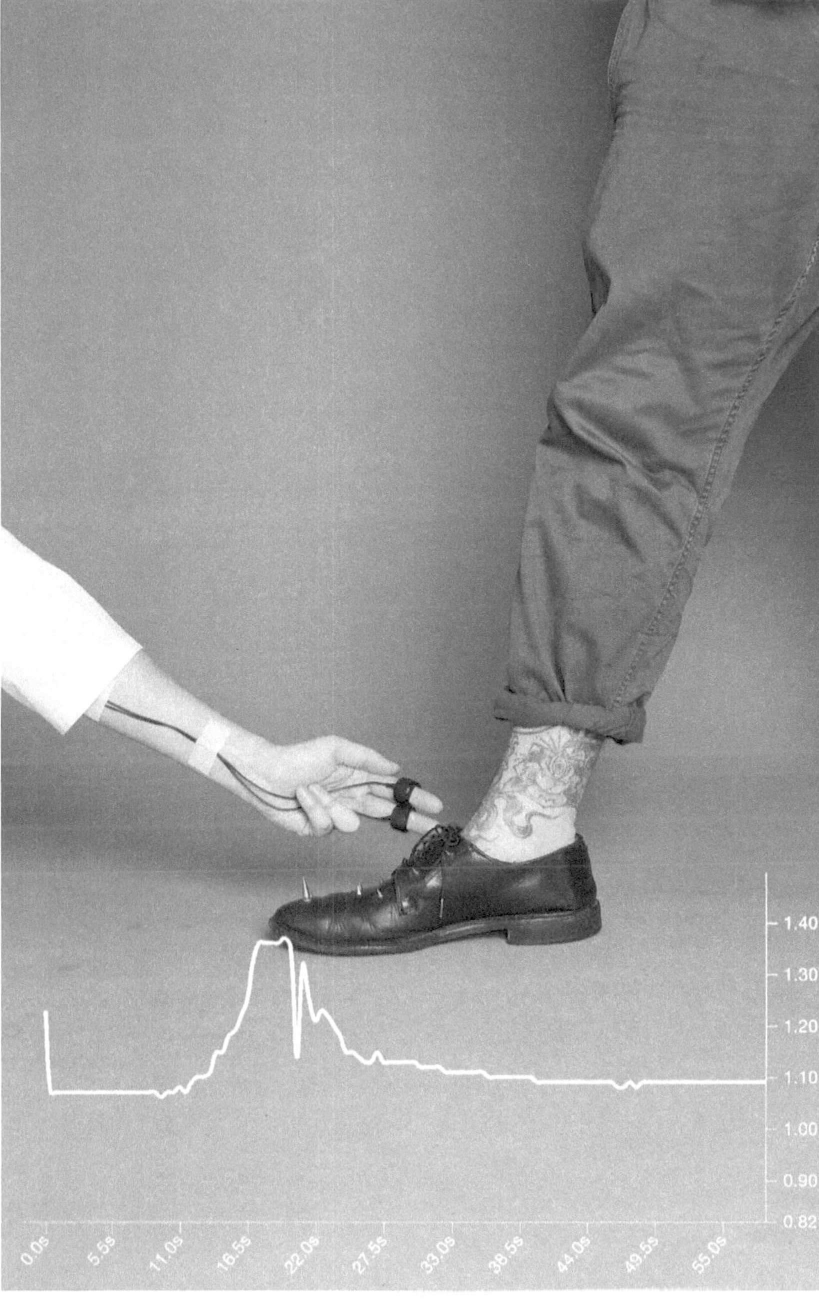

1.40
1.30
1.20
1.10
1.00
0.90
0.82
0.0s
5.5s
11.0s
16.5s
22.0s
27.5s
33.0s
38.5s
44.0s
49.5s
55.0s

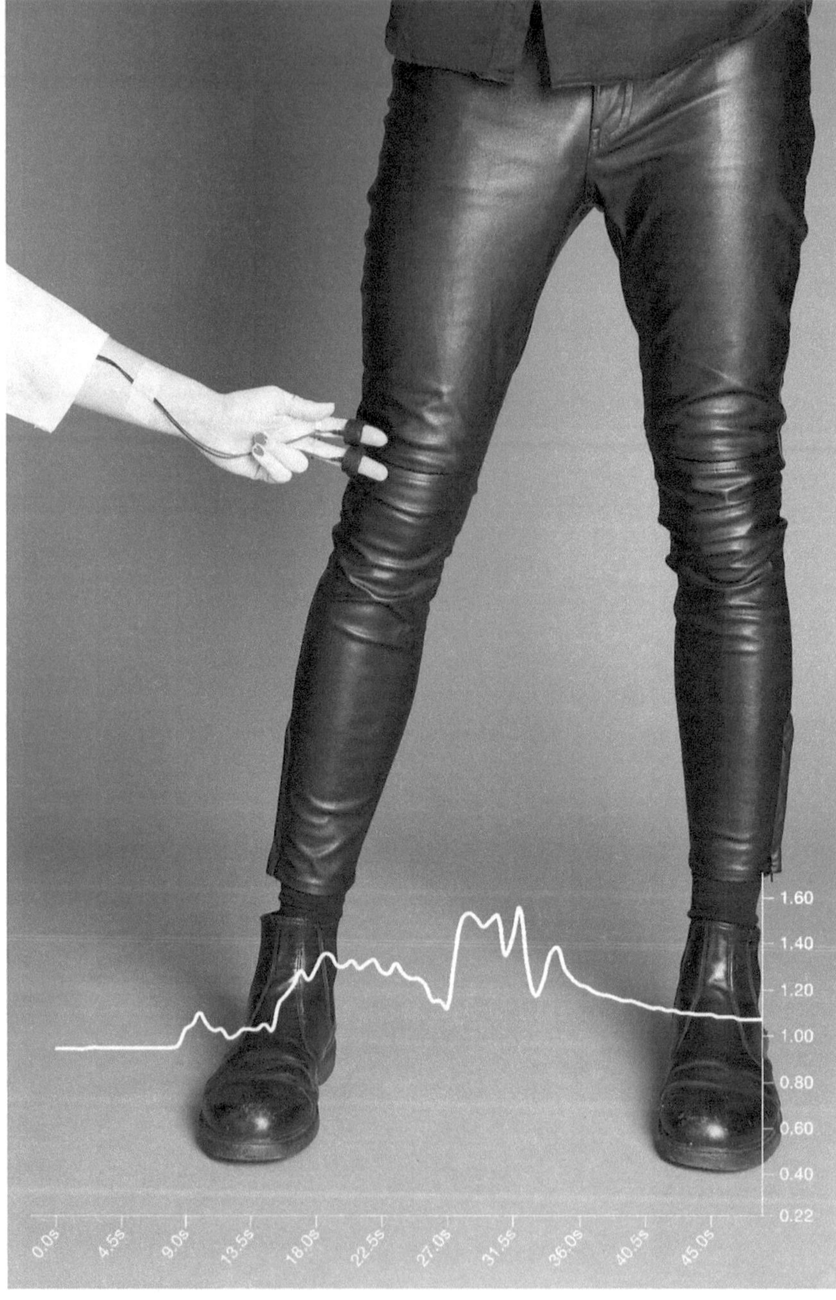

1.60
1.40
1.20
1.00
0.80
0.60
0.40
0.22
0.0s
4.5s
9.0s
13.5s
18.0s
22.5s
27.0s
31.5s
36.0s
40.5s
45.0s

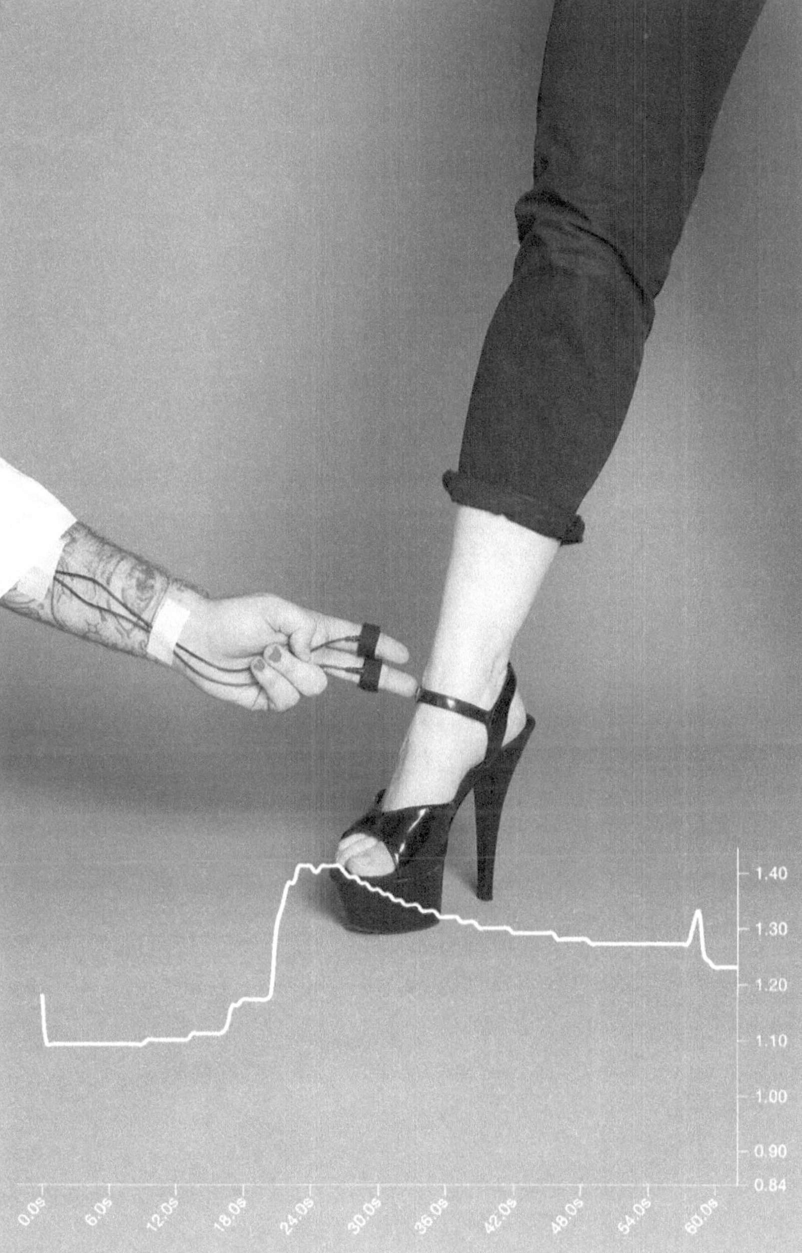

1.40
1.30
1.20
1.10
1.00
0.90
0.84
0.0s
6.0s
12.0s
18.0s
24.0s
30.0s
36.0s
42.0s
48.0s
54.0s
60.0s

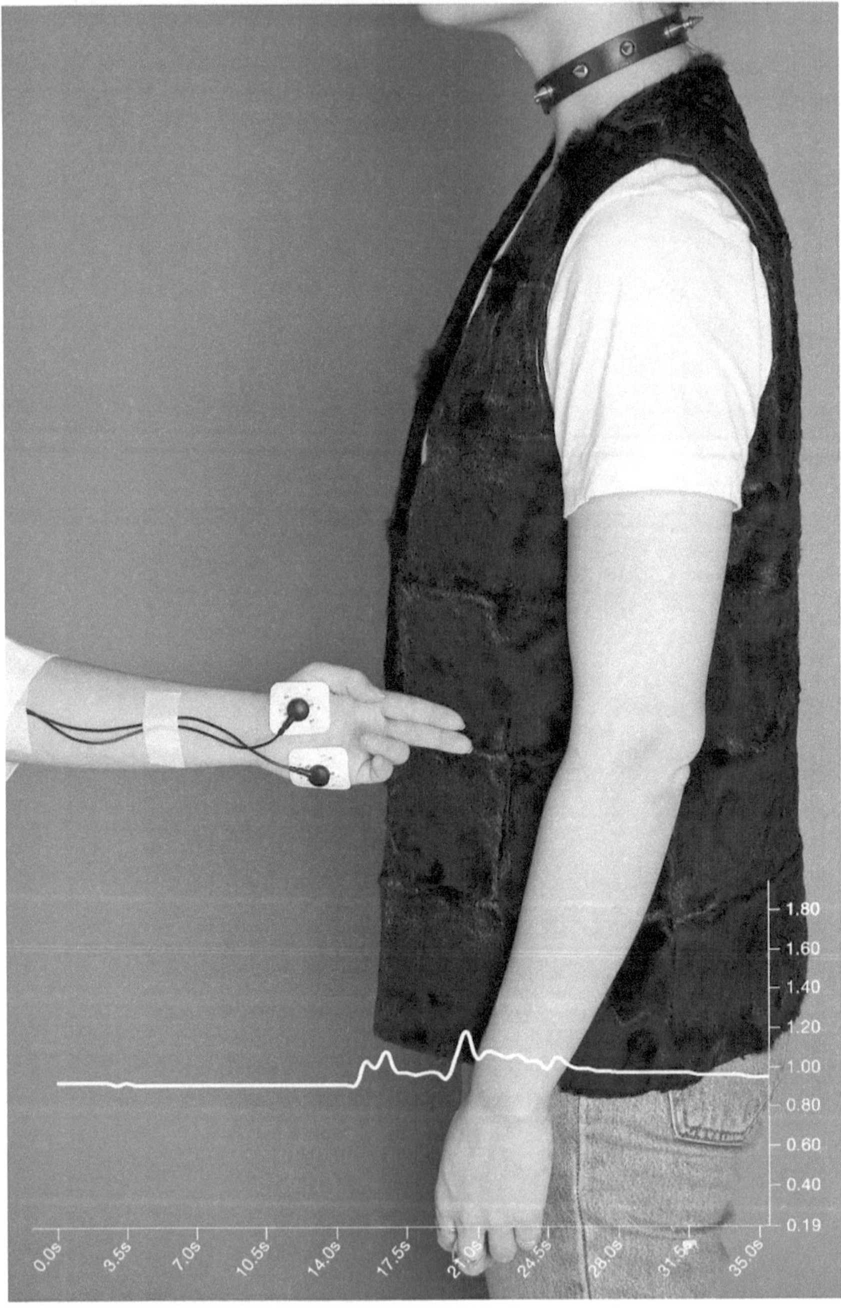

1.80
1.60
1.40
1.20
1.00
0.80
0.60
0.40
0.19
0.0s
3.5s
7.0s
10.5s
14.0s
17.5s
21.0s
24.5s
28.0s
31.5s
35.0s

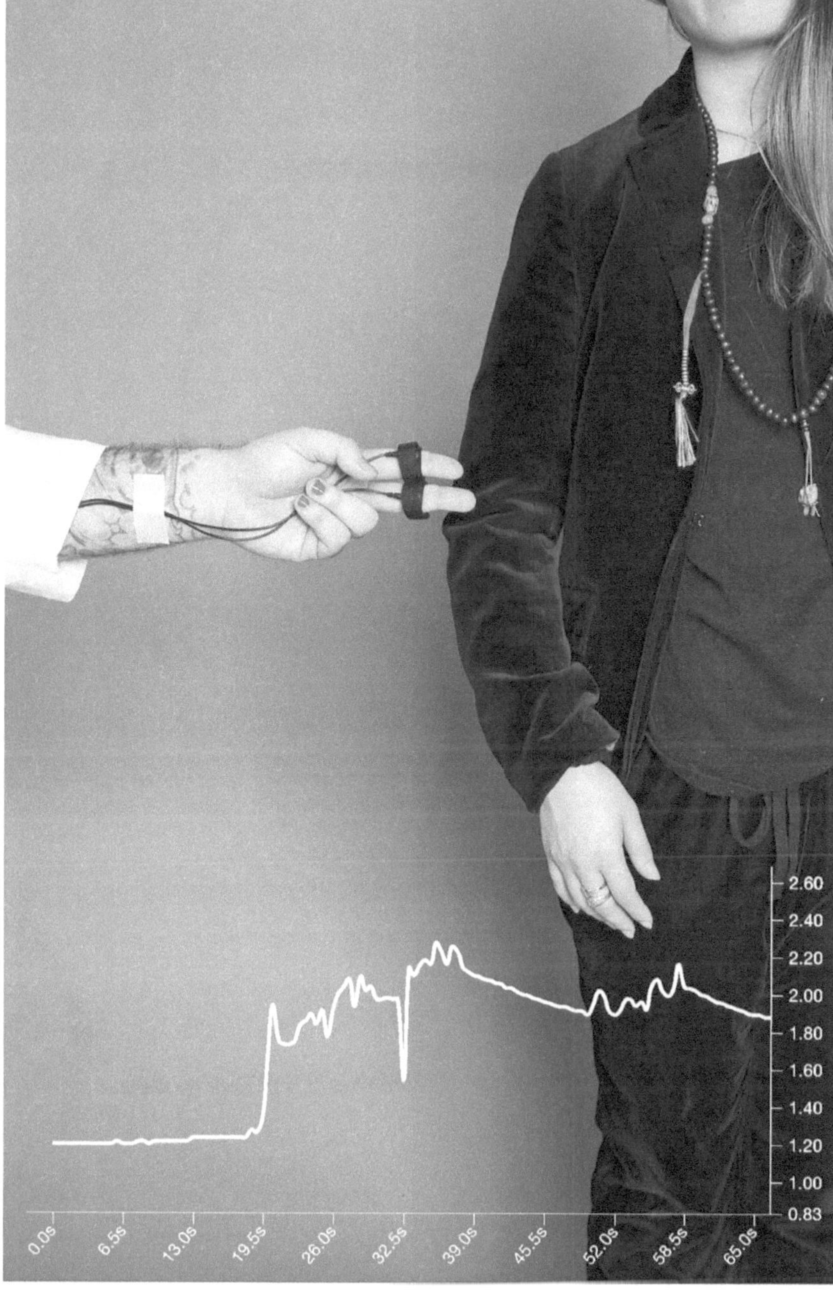
2.60
2.40
2.20
2.00
1.80
1.60
1.40
1.20
1.00
0.83
0.0s
6.5s
13.0s
19.5s
26.0s
32.5s
39.0s
45.5s
52.0s
58.5s
65.0s

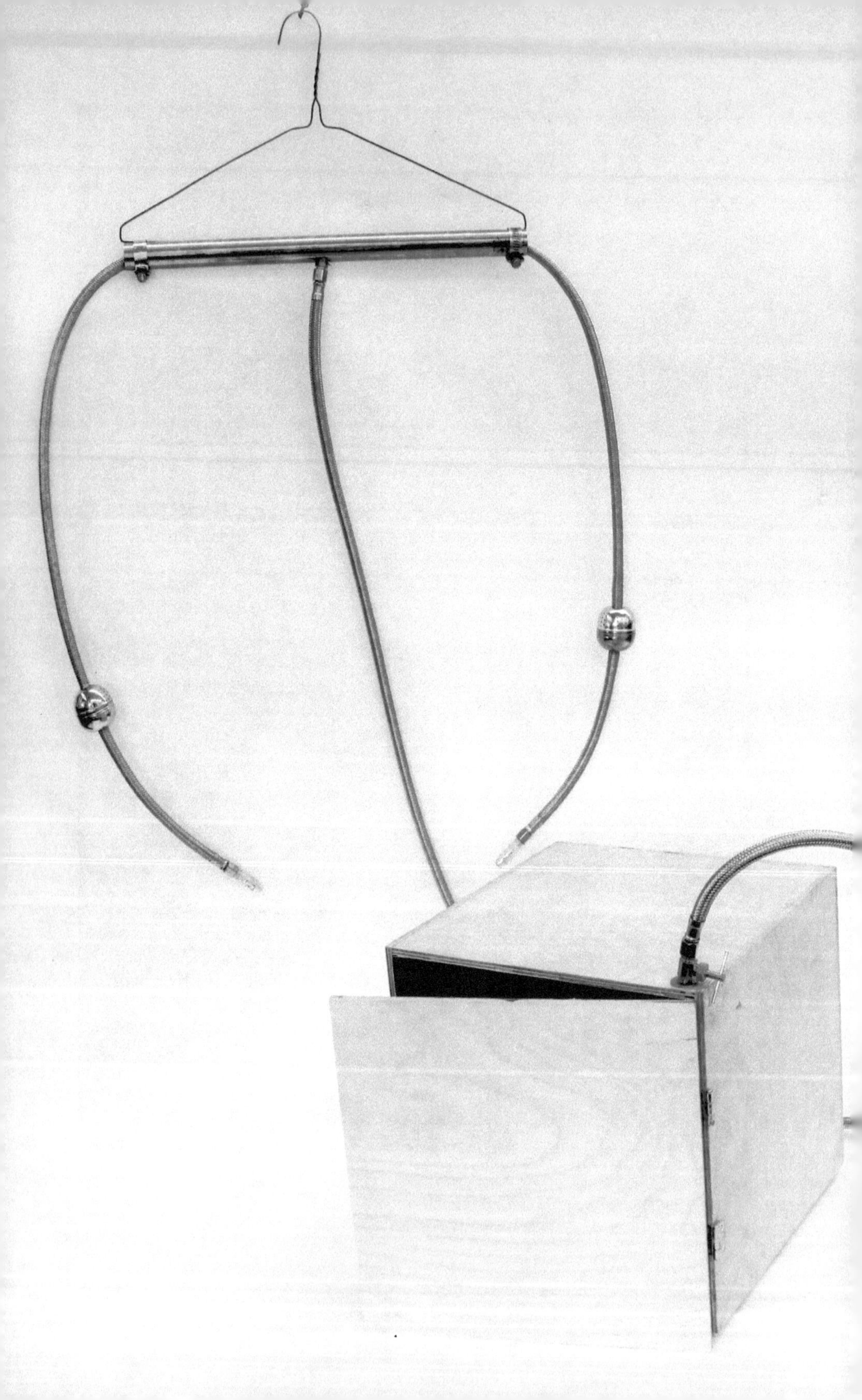

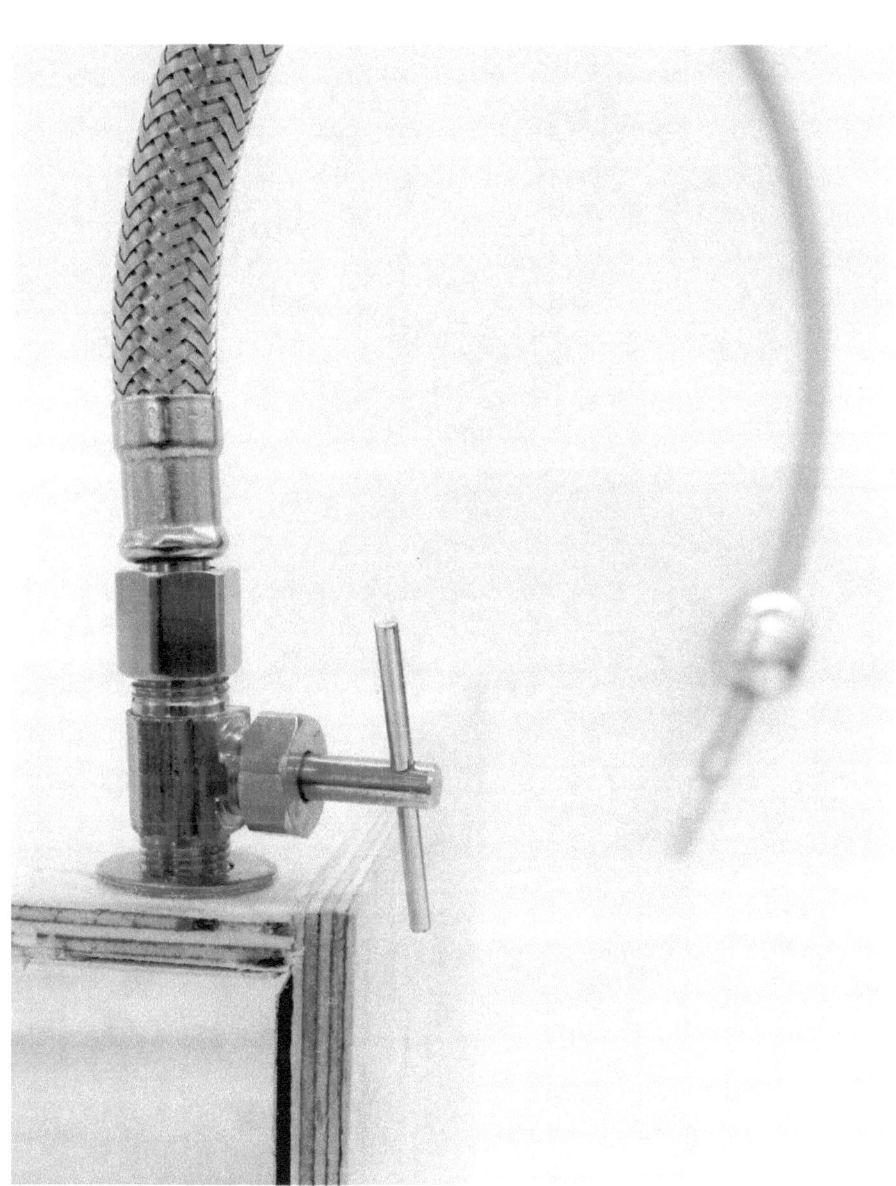

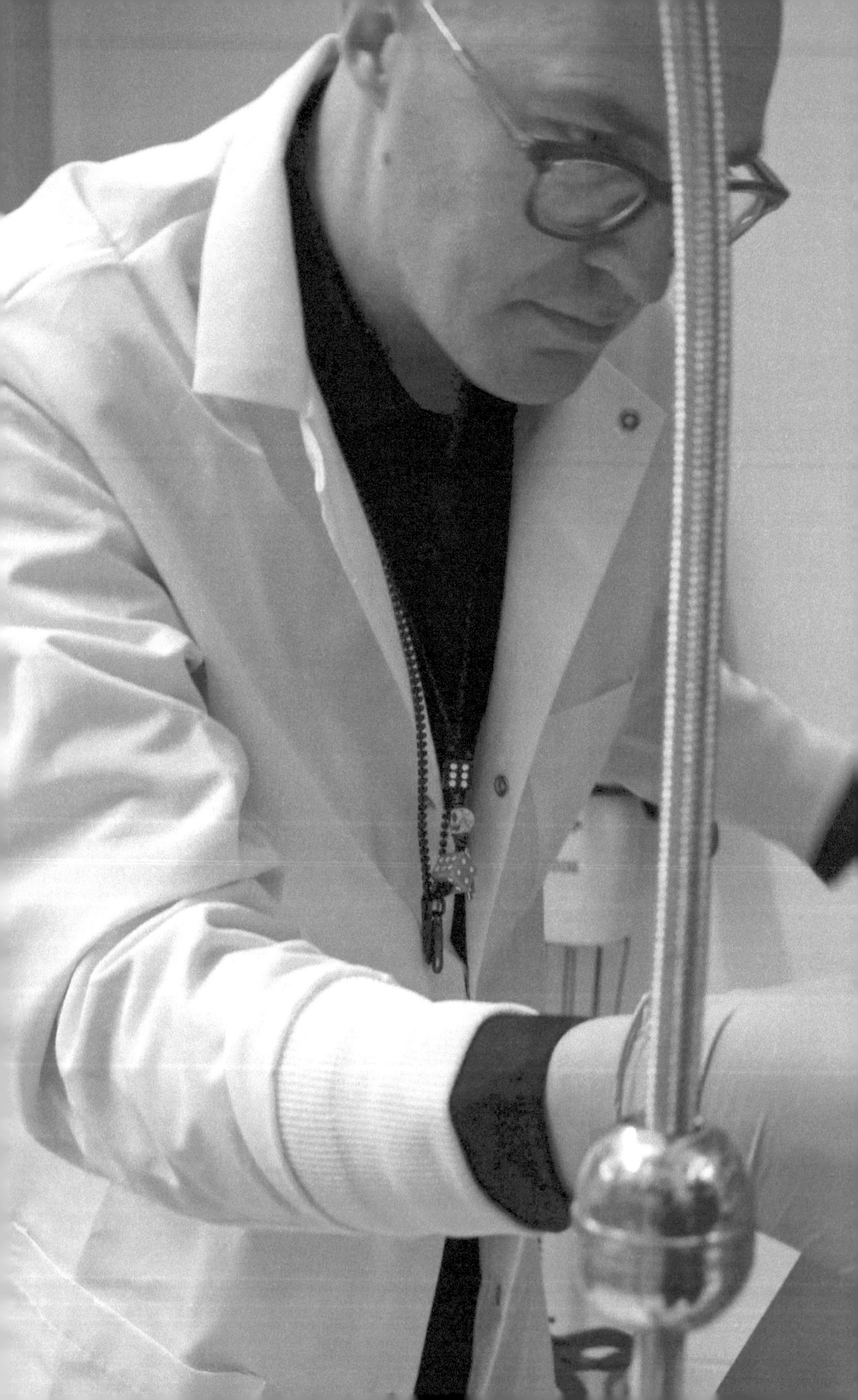

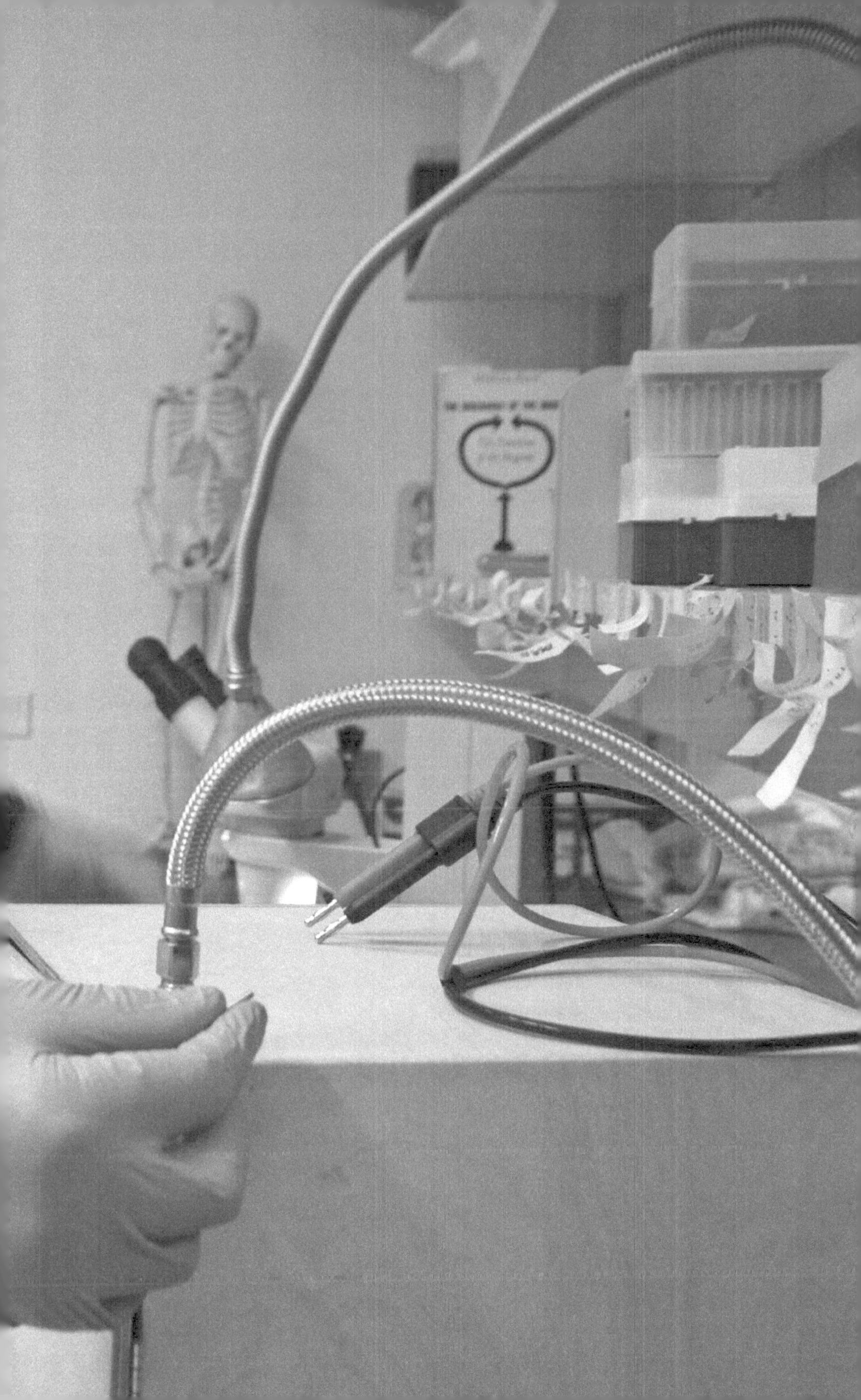

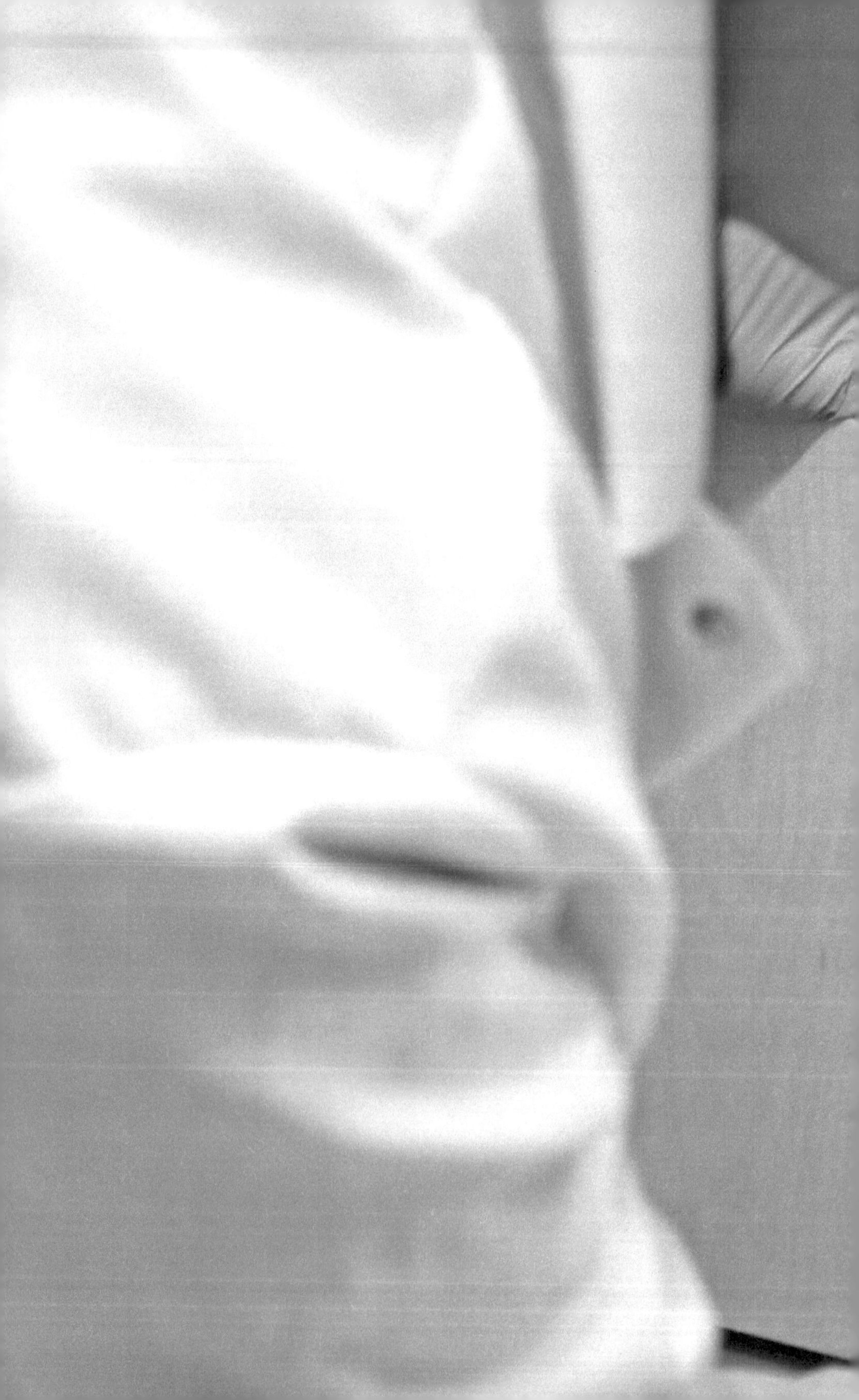

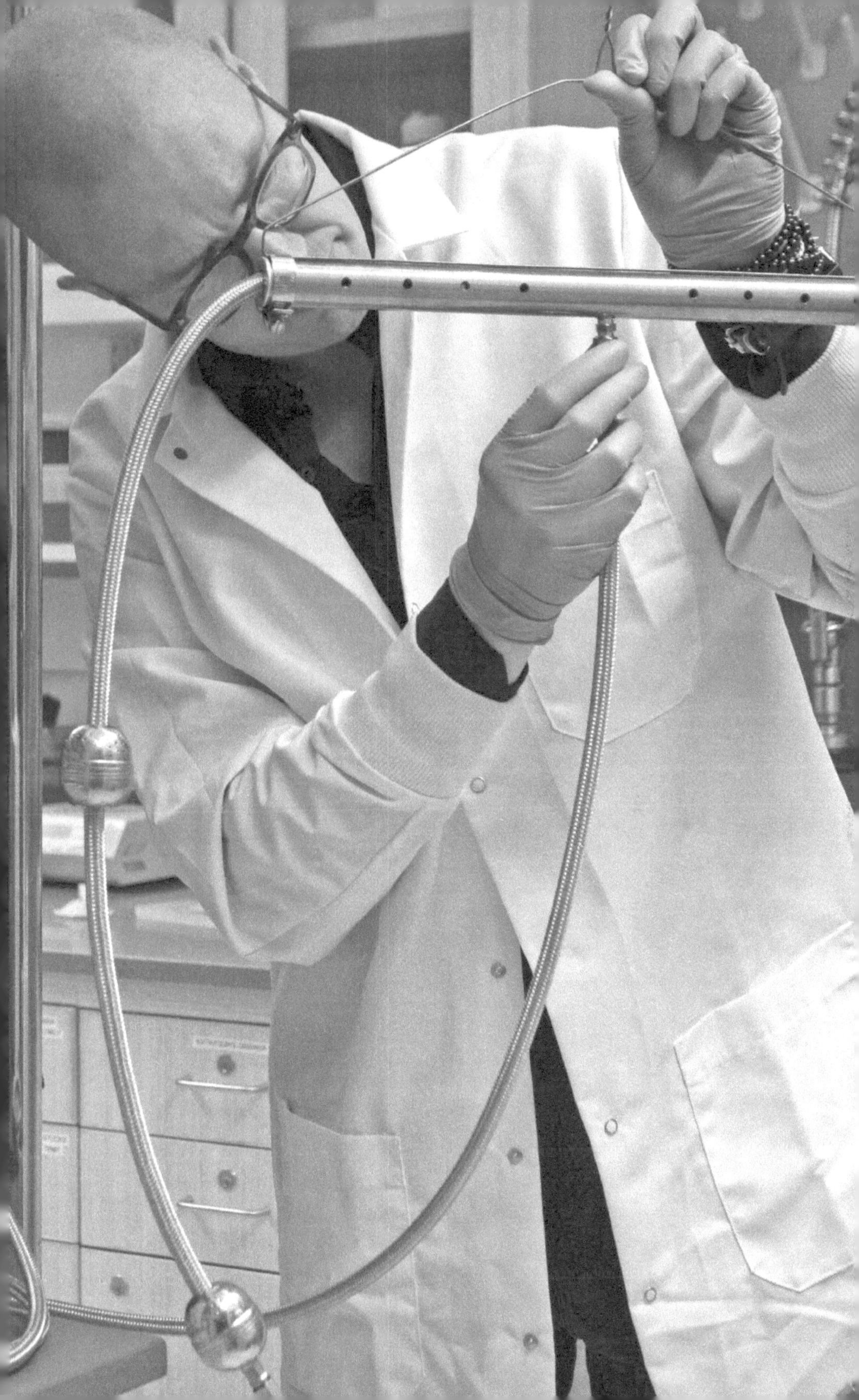

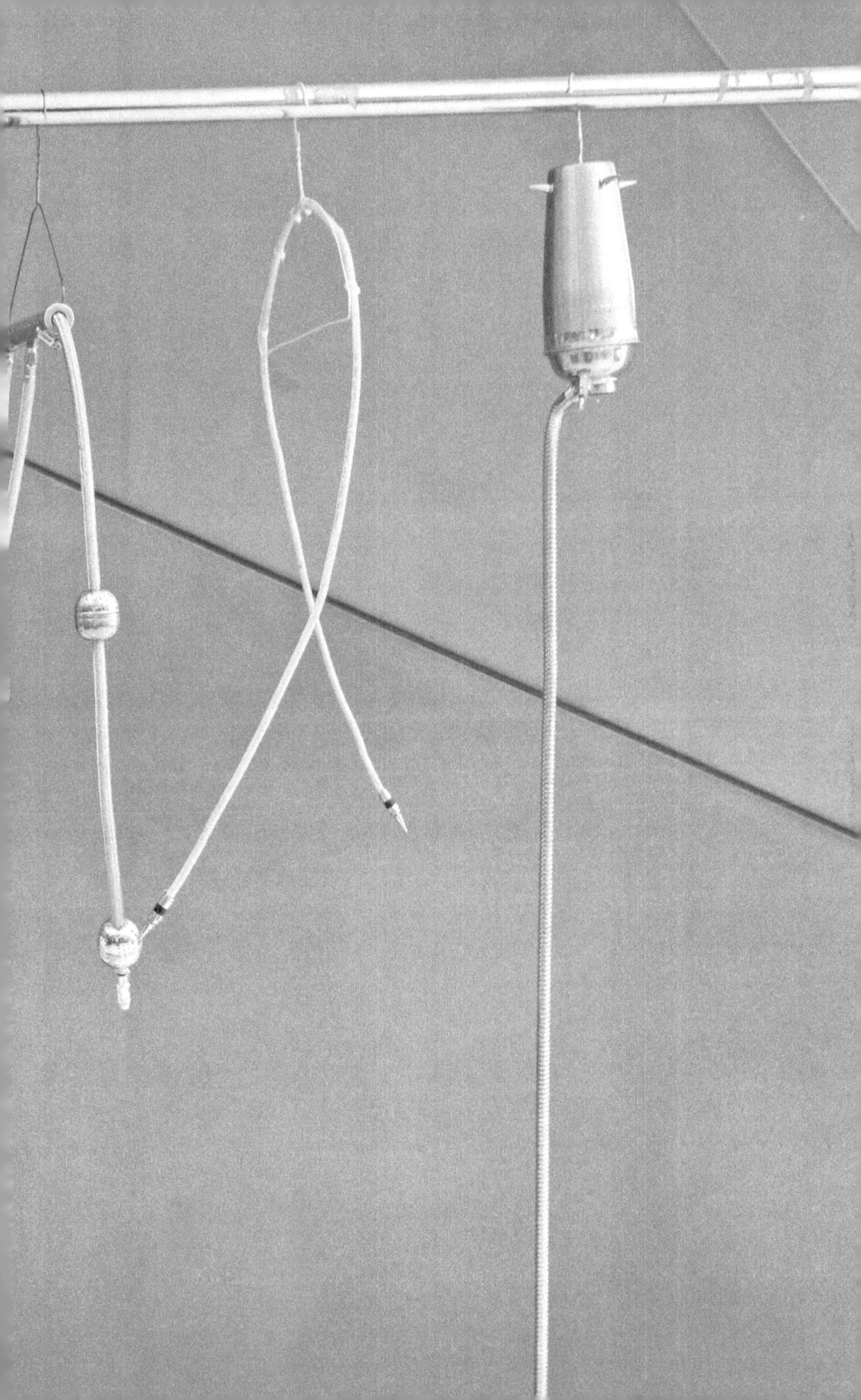

PROJECT EXHIBITION

V⊥TAL VOGUE

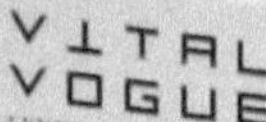

Curated by Otto von Busch
March 24 – April 4, 2014

THE psychoanalyst, political theorist, biologist, and pioneer of body therapies Wilhelm Reich was one of Freud's most promising but also controversial students. After the Nazi takeover in Germany in 1933, Reich fled to Norway, but was exiled again and came to New York in the fall of 1939 after being invited to teach at The New School for Social Research. A renowned psychoanalyst and researcher, Reich presented his psychosomatic and biosocial work in the course "Character Formation: Biological and Sociological Aspects." During his time at The New School, Reich continued his lab research on bioelectrical energy, what he called orgone, and came to focus on the connection between cancer and the blocked flow of life energy in the patient's body. Reich's contract at The New School was not renewed, as Alvin Johnson, the director of The New School, argued the school was no medical college.

Taking inspiration from Reich, fashion can be understood as a biological as much as social phenomenon; when fashion works at its best, we feel it in our bodies. The agency of fashion is not in the system, but in your body. But we can also come to fear the pain of failure, thus seeking safe choices, asking designers to lead us, that in turn aggravate our submission.

The exhibition inside the gallery makes you a co-researcher in our lab, interpreting how Reich's ideas could be applied within the realm of fashion.

Objects (left to right):

1. Hiring letter for Reich (1939) from the archives of the Orgone Institute. By permission of the Wilhelm Reich Infant Trust.

2. Course catalogue from The New School (1940) from The New School Archives and Special Collections.

3. Letter discontinuing Reich's teaching at The New School (1941) from the archives of the Orgone Institute. By permission of the Wilhelm Reich Infant Trust.

4. Pages from Reich lecture notes from his course "Character Formation: Biological and Sociological Aspects" (1940) from the archives of the Orgone Institute. By permission of the Wilhelm Reich Infant Trust.

DISCLAIMER

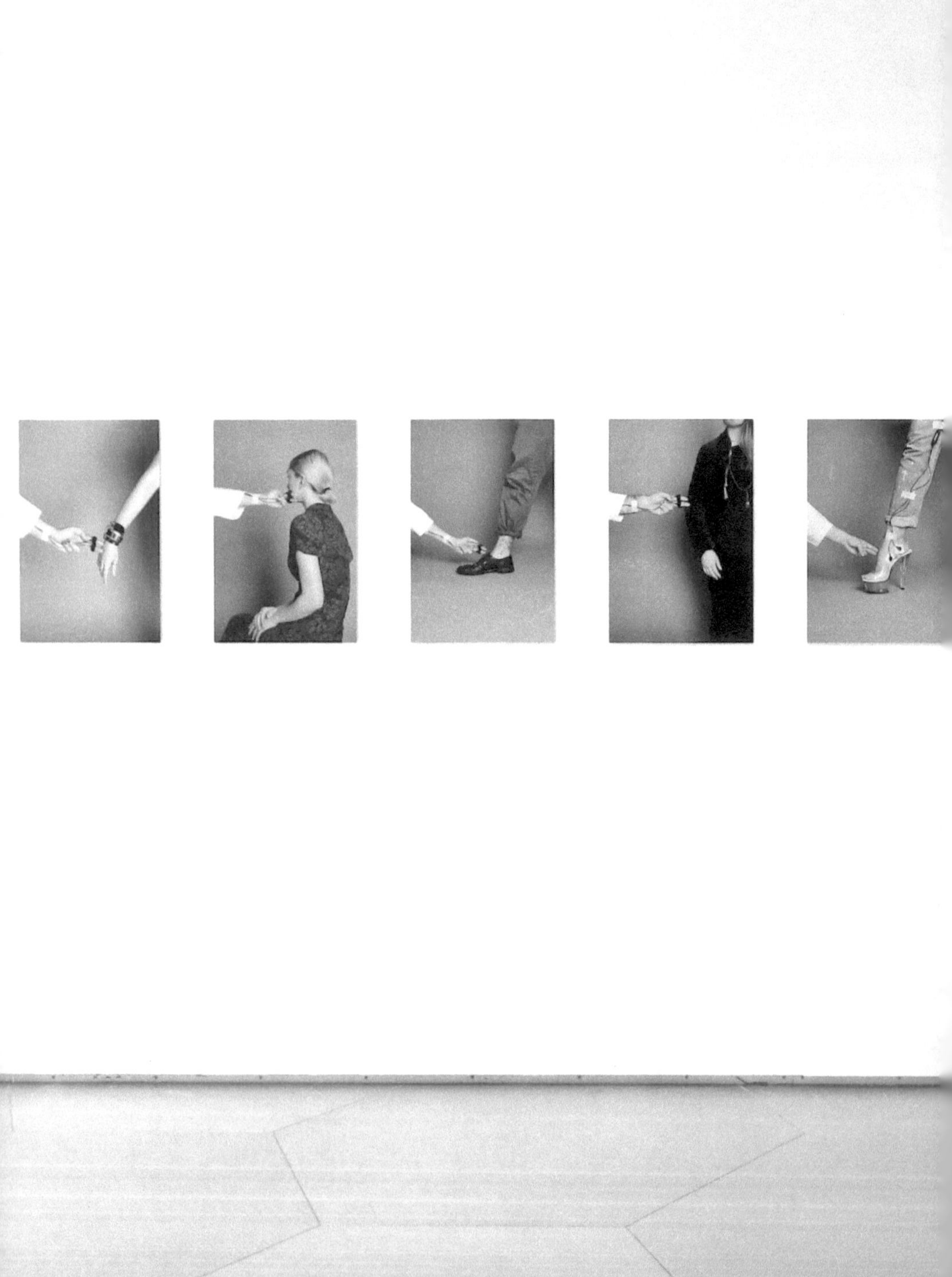

PLAGUE
WE ARE
BORN FREE
BUT EVERYWHERE
HELD IN
CHAIN STORES
EROS
SOCIAL

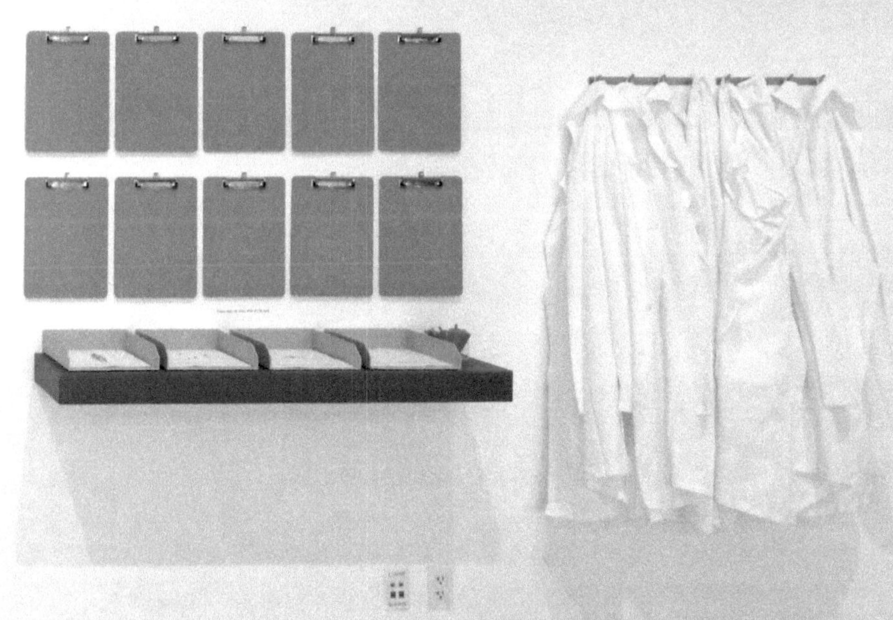

Wilhelm Reich
THE DISCOVERY OF THE ORGONE
The Function
of the Orgasm
Noonday 219 $2.95

of the living is a threat only to *one* attitude and to *one* kind of social and moral order: *the authoritarian dictatorial regime of any kind, which, by means of compulsive morality and a compulsive attitude toward work, attempts to destroy spontaneous decency and natural self-regulation of the vital forces.*

It is time to be honest: authoritarian dictatorship exists not only in totalitarian states. It is found in the church as well as in academic organizations, among the Communists as well as in parliamentary governments. It is a general human tendency which owes its existence to the suppression of the living function; it forms, in all nations, the mass-psychological basis for the acceptance and establishment of dictatorship. Its basic elements are mystification of the life process; actual helplessness, material and social; fear of the responsibility for shaping one's own life; and, consequently, the craving for illusory security and for authority, passive or active. The age-old, *genuine* striving for a democratization of social life is based on self-determination, on *natural* sociality and morality, on *joyful* work and *earthly* happiness in love. People with this striving consider any illusion a danger. Thus, they will not only be unafraid of the scientific comprehension of the living function, but they will put it to use in mastering decisive problems pertaining to the formation of human character structure; in so doing, they will be able to master these problems in a scientific and practical, instead of in an illusionary manner. Everywhere people are striving to turn formal democracy into a true democracy of all those engaged in productive work, into a *work democracy*,[1] that is, a democracy on the basis of a *natural* organization of the work process.

In the field of mental hygiene, it is a matter of the tremendous task of replacing sexual chaos, prostitution, porno-

---

[1] Cf. Glossary, "work democracy".

graphic literature and sexual racketeering with natural happiness in love, guaranteed by society. This does not imply any intention of "destroying the family" or of "undermining morals". In fact, *family and morals are already undermined by the compulsive family and compulsive morality.* Professionally, we are confronted with the task of repairing the damage done by sexual and familial chaos, in the form of mental disease. If we are to be able to master this psychic plague, we have to distinguish sharply between what is natural love between parents and children, and what is familial compulsion. The universal disease *"familitis"* destroys all that honest human endeavor attempts to bring about.

Though I do not belong to any political or religious organization, I have, nevertheless, a definite concept of social living. This concept is—in contrast to all varieties of political, purely ideological or mystical philosophy—*scientifically rational.* According to this concept, I believe that there will be no lasting peace on our earth, and that all attempts to socialize human beings will be in vain, as long as politicians and dictators of one kind or another, who have not the slightest awareness of the actualities of the life process, continue to lead masses of people who are endemically neurotic and sexually sick. The natural function of the socialization of the human is that of guaranteeing work and natural fulfillment in love. These two biological activities of man have always depended upon scientific searching and thinking. *Knowledge, work and natural love are the sources of life. They should also be the forces that govern our life,* the complete responsibility for these being carried by all who are producing by their labor.

If we are asked whether we are for or against democracy, our answer is: We are for democracy, unequivocally and without compromise. But—we are for a genuine democracy, for a democracy in real life, not a democracy on paper. We

He who disputes this right of the scientist, the physician, the teacher, the technician or the writer, and calls himself a democrat, is a hypocrite, or at least a victim of the plague of irrationalism. The struggle against the plague of dictatorship is hopeless without determination and without a serious concern with problems of the life process; for, dictatorship lives—and can only live—in the darkness of *unresolved* problems of the life process. Man is helpless where he lacks knowledge; this helplessness born of ignorance forms the fertile soil for dictatorship. A social order cannot be called democratic if it is afraid of raising decisive questions, of finding unexpected answers, or of the clash of opinions regarding them. If it has such fears, it tumbles under the slightest attack upon its institutions by would-be dictators. This is what happened in Europe.

"Freedom of worship" is dictatorship so long as there is, at the same time, no *freedom of science,* and, consequently, no free competition in the interpretation of the life process. We must once and for all decide whether "God" is an all-powerful, bearded figure in heaven or the cosmic law of nature governing us. Only when God and natural law are identical, can science and religion be reconciled. There is but one step from the dictatorship of those who represent God on earth to that of those who want to replace him on earth.

Morality is also dictatorship if it results in considering people with a natural feeling for life as on the same level with pornography. Whether it wants to or not, it thus prolongs the existence of smut and brings ruin to natural happiness in love. It is necessary to raise a sharp protest against calling a man immoral who bases his social behavior on inner laws instead of external compulsive forms. People are man and wife not because they have received the sacrament but because they feel themselves man and wife. The inner and not the external law is the yardstick of genuine

freedom. Moralistic hypocrisy is the most dangerous enemy of natural morality. Moralistic hypocrisy cannot be fought with another kind of compulsive morality, but only with the knowledge of the natural law of the sexual process. *Natural moral behavior presupposes freedom of the natural sexual process.* Conversely, compulsive morality and pathological sexuality go hand in hand.

The line of compulsion is the line of least resistance. It is easier to demand discipline and to enforce it by authority than it is to bring up children to a joyful initiative in their work and to natural sexual behavior. It is easier to declare oneself an omniscient, God-sent Führer and to decree what millions of people should think and do, than it is to expose oneself to the struggle between the rational and irrational in the clash of opinions. It is easier to insist on legally required performance of respect and love than it is to win friendship through genuinely decent behavior. It is easier to sell one's independence for economic security than it is to lead an independent, responsible existence and to be master of oneself. It is easier to dictate to subordinates what they ought to do than it is to *guide* them while respecting their own individuality. This is why dictatorship is always easier than *true* democracy. This is why the indolent democratic leader envies the dictator, and tries, in his inadequate way, to imitate him. It is easy to represent the commonplace, and difficult to represent the truth.

He who does not have confidence in that which is alive, or has lost it, easily falls prey to the subterranean fear of life which begets dictatorship. *That which is alive is in itself reasonable.* It becomes a caricature when it is not allowed to live. If it is a caricature, life can only create terror. This is why knowledge of that which is alive can alone banish terror.

Whatever the outcome of the bloody struggles of our disjointed world may be for the coming centuries: the science

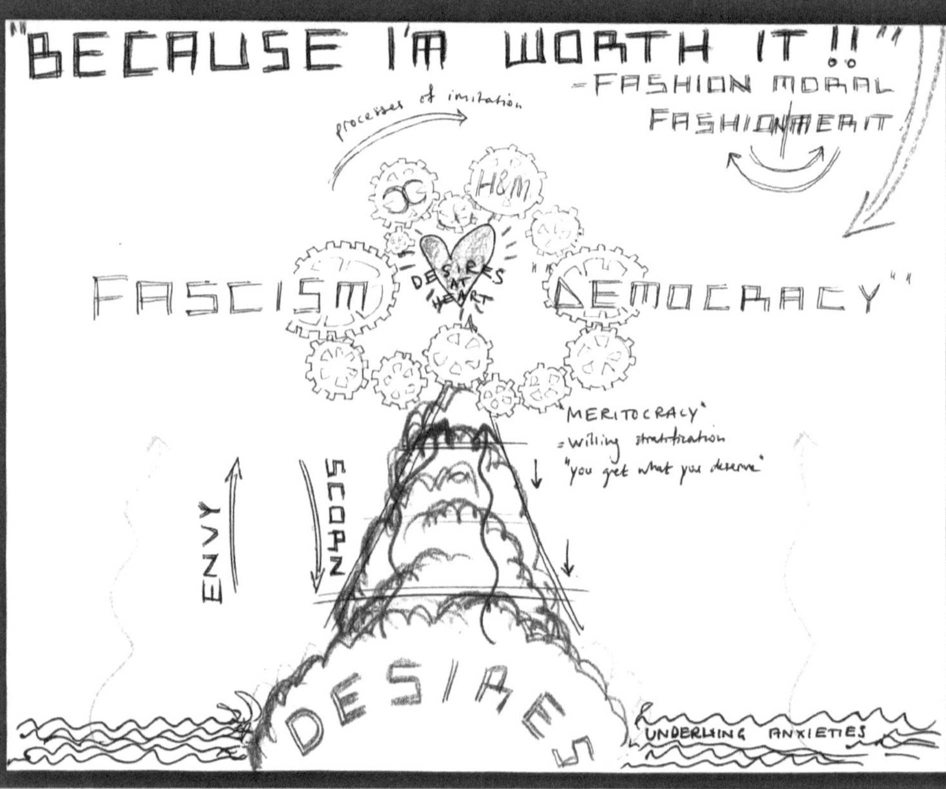

Chapter III

GAPS IN THE THEORY OF SEX AND IN PSYCHOLOGY

1. "PLEASURE" AND "INSTINCT"

On the basis of my biological studies, and against the background of Freud's definition of instinct, I tackled a certain difficulty in the theory of the pleasure principle. According to Freud, there existed the peculiar phenomenon that *sexual* tension—in contrast to the general nature of tension—was of a pleasurable nature. According to customary concepts, tension could be *only unpleasurable*, and only release of tension could bring pleasure. My interpretation of this phenomenon was as follows: During sexual preliminaries a tension is created which would be experienced as unpleasurable if it were not followed by gratification. However, the anticipation of the pleasure of gratification produces not only tension, but also discharges a *small* quantity of sexual energy. This partial satisfaction, plus the anticipation of the great end-pleasure, outweighs the unpleasure of the initial tension. This interpretation was the beginning of my later functional theory of sexual activity. I came to see in the instinct nothing but the "*motor aspect of pleasure*". Modern psychological science had given up the concept that our perceptions are nothing but passive experiences, and had replaced it by the more correct concept that each perception

32

is based on an *active* attitude of the ego toward the sensation or the stimulus ("Wahrnehmungs*intention*", "Wahrnehmungs*akt*"). This was an important step ahead, for now one could understand how the same stimulus which in one case produces a sensation of pleasure, may, in another case—with a different inner attitude—not be perceived at all. The sexological significance of this is that a gentle stroking at an erogenous zone may result in a pleasurable sensation in one individual, whereas this may be absent in another individual who feels only a touching or rubbing. This was the beginning of the differentiation between full orgastic pleasure and pure tactile sensations, or, fundamentally, the differentiation of *orgastic potency* from *orgastic impotence*. Those who are acquainted with my electro-biological research will realize that the "active attitude of the ego toward perception" is identical with the flowing of the electric charge of the organism toward the periphery.

Thus, pleasure had an active motor and a passive sensory component, both of which are fused into one. The motor component of pleasure is experienced passively at the same time as the sensory component is actively perceived. At that time, scientific thinking was rather complicated, but good. Later I learned to formulate it more simply: A drive is no longer something that exists *here* and seeks pleasure *there*, but *it is motor pleasure itself*.

Here was a gap: How was one to explain the urge for repetition of pleasure that had once been experienced? I remembered Semon's theory of the engrams and made the following formulation: *The sexual drive is nothing but the motor memory of previously experienced pleasure*. The concept of drives became thus *reduced to the concept of pleasure*.

There remained the question as to the *nature* of pleasure. With the false modesty in vogue at that time I pronounced a "semper ignorabimus". Nevertheless, I continued to strug-

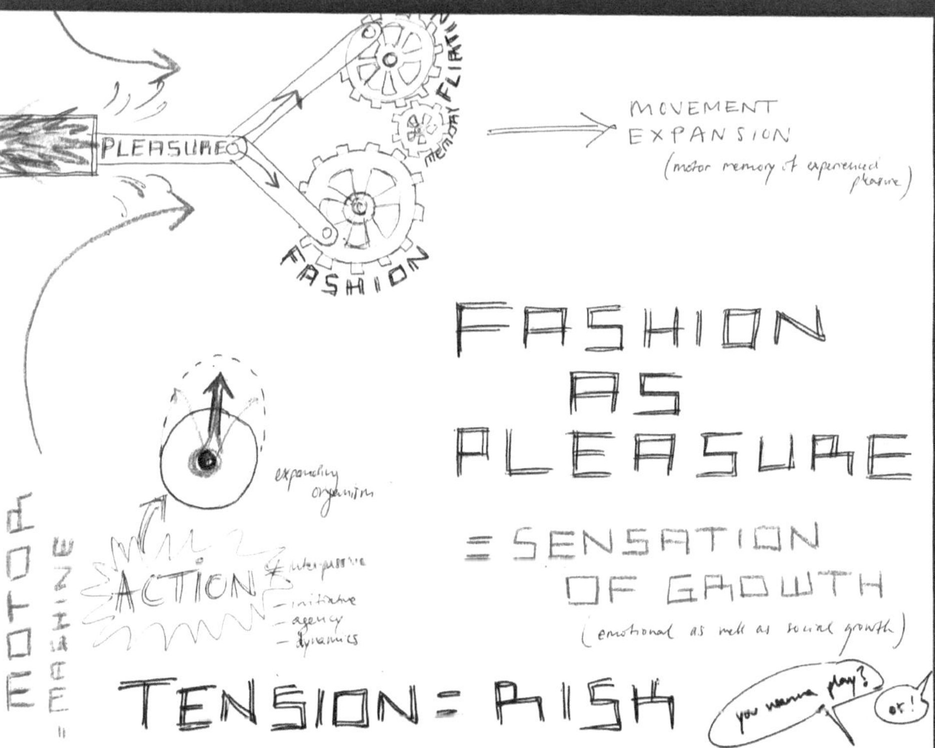

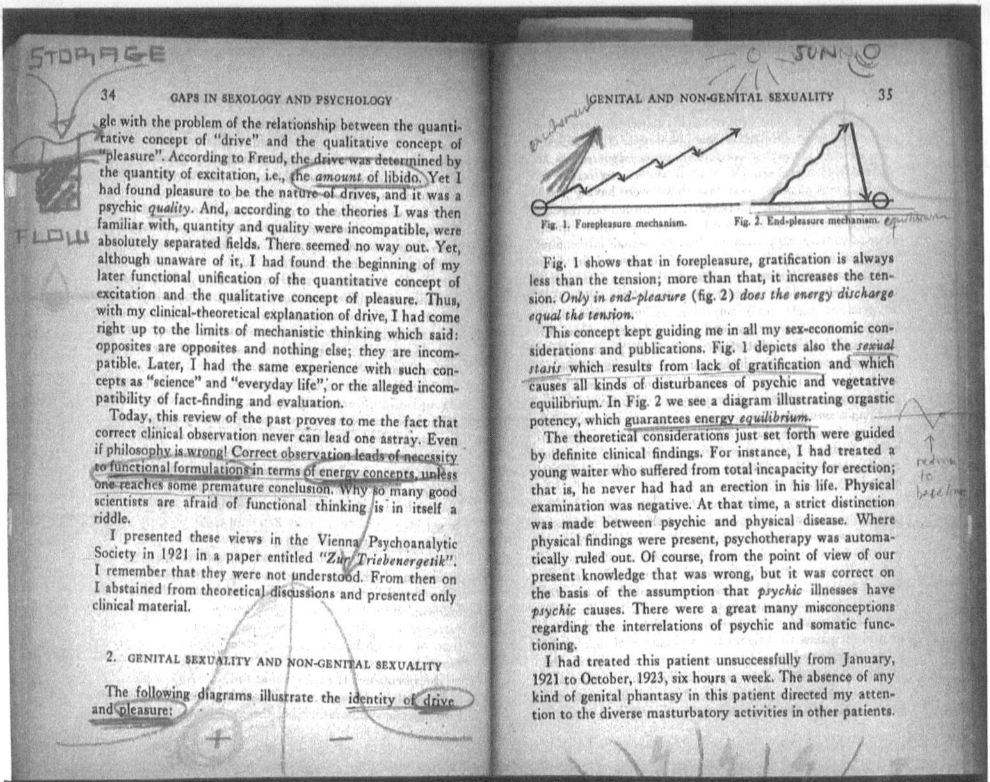

gle with the problem of the relationship between the quantitative concept of "drive" and the qualitative concept of
"pleasure". According to Freud, the drive was determined by
the quantity of excitation, i.e., the *amount* of libido. Yet I
had found pleasure to be the nature of drives, and it was a
psychic *quality*. And, according to the theories I was then
familiar with, quantity and quality were incompatible, were
absolutely separated fields. There seemed no way out. Yet,
although unaware of it, I had found the beginning of my
later functional unification of the quantitative concept of
excitation and the qualitative concept of pleasure. Thus,
with my clinical-theoretical explanation of drive, I had come
right up to the limits of mechanistic thinking which said:
opposites are opposites and nothing else; they are incompatible. Later, I had the same experience with such concepts as "science" and "everyday life", or the alleged incom-
patibility of fact-finding and evaluation.

Today, this review of the past proves to me the fact that
correct clinical observation never can lead one astray. Even
if philosophy is wrong! Correct observation leads of necessity
to functional formulations in terms of energy concepts, unless
one reaches some premature conclusion. Why so many good
scientists are afraid of functional thinking is in itself a
riddle.

I presented these views in the Vienna Psychoanalytic
Society in 1921 in a paper entitled *"Zur Triebenergetik"*.
I remember that they were not understood. From then on
I abstained from theoretical discussions and presented only
clinical material.

2. GENITAL SEXUALITY AND NON-GENITAL SEXUALITY

The following diagrams illustrate the identity of drive
and pleasure:

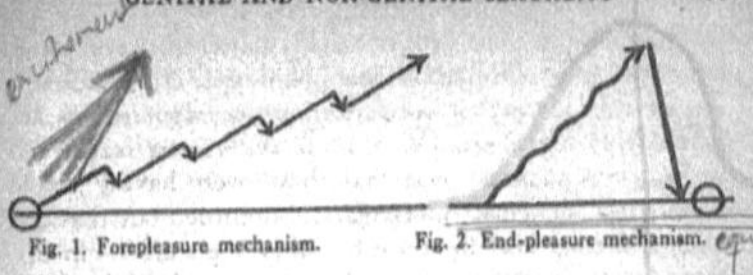

Fig. 1. Forepleasure mechanism.   Fig. 2. End-pleasure mechanism.

Fig. 1 shows that in forepleasure, gratification is always
less than the tension; more than that, it increases the tension. *Only in end-pleasure* (fig. 2) *does the energy discharge
equal the tension.*

This concept kept guiding me in all my sex-economic considerations and publications. Fig. 1 depicts also the *sexual
stasis* which results from lack of gratification and which
causes all kinds of disturbances of psychic and vegetative
equilibrium. In Fig. 2 we see a diagram illustrating orgastic
potency, which guarantees energy *equilibrium*.

The theoretical considerations just set forth were guided
by definite clinical findings. For instance, I had treated a
young waiter who suffered from total incapacity for erection;
that is, he never had had an erection in his life. Physical
examination was negative. At that time, a strict distinction
was made between psychic and physical disease. Where
physical findings were present, psychotherapy was automatically ruled out. Of course, from the point of view of our
present knowledge that was wrong, but it was correct on
the basis of the assumption that *psychic* illnesses have
psychic causes. There were a great many misconceptions
regarding the interrelations of psychic and somatic functioning.

I had treated this patient unsuccessfully from January,
1921 to October, 1923, six hours a week. The absence of any
kind of genital phantasy in this patient directed my attention to the diverse masturbatory activities in other patients.

thing was wrong with natural science. For, Wundt and his pupils knew nothing of the human in his living reality. They evaluated him according to the number of seconds he needed to react to the word "dog". They still do. We, on the other hand, evaluated a person according to the manner in which he handled his conflicts in life, and the motives which activated him. To me, there loomed behind this argument the more important question as to whether it might be possible to arrive at a concrete formulation of Freud's concept of *psychic energy*, or whether it might be possible even to subsume it under the general concept of energy.

Philosophical arguments cannot be countered with facts. The Viennese philosopher and physiologist Allers refused to enter upon the question of the existence of an unconscious psychic life, on the grounds that the assumption of an "unconscious" was *a priori* erroneous from a philosophical point of view". I hear similar objections today. When I assert that highly sterilized substances produce life, it is argued that the slide was dirty, or that, if there seems to be life, it is "only a matter of Brownian movement". The fact that it is very easy to distinguish dirt on the slide from the bions, and equally easy to distinguish Brownian movement from vegetative movement, is not taken into consideration. In brief, "objective science" is a problem in itself.

In this confusion, I was unexpectedly aided by such everyday clinical observations as the ones provided by the two patients mentioned above. Gradually it became clear that *the intensity of an idea depends upon the quantity of the somatic excitation with which it is connected.* Emotions originate from the instincts, consequently from the *somatic* sphere. Ideas, on the other hand, certainly are a definitely "psychic", "non-somatic" thing. *What, then, is the connection between the "non-somatic" idea and the "somatic" excitation?* For example, the idea of sexual intercourse is vivid and forceful if one is in a state of full sexual excitation. For

some other time after sexual gratification, however, it cannot be vividly reproduced; it is dim, colorless and vague. Just here must the secret of the interrelation between the "*physiogenic*" anxiety neurosis and the "psychogenic" psychoneurosis be hidden. The first patient temporarily lost all his psychic compulsion symptoms after he had experienced sexual gratification; with the return of sexual excitation, they recurred and lasted until the next occasion of gratification. The second patient, on the other hand, had meticulously worked through everything in the psychic realm, but in him, sexual excitation remained absent; the unconscious ideas at the root of his erective impotence had not been touched by the treatment.

Things began to take shape. I began to understand that an idea, endowed with a very small amount of energy, was capable of provoking an *increase* of excitation. The excitation thus provoked, in turn made the idea vivid and forceful. If the excitation subsided, the idea would collapse also. If, as is the case in the stasis neurosis, the idea of sexual intercourse does not arise in consciousness, due to moral inhibition, the excitation attaches itself to other ideas which are less subject to censorship. From this, I concluded: the stasis neurosis is a *somatic* disturbance, caused by sexual excitation which is misdirected because it is frustrated. However, *without a psychic inhibition, sexual energy can never become misdirected.* I was surprised that Freud had overlooked this fact. Once an inhibition has created the sexual stasis, this in turn may easily increase the inhibition and reactivate infantile ideas which then take the place of normal ones. That is, infantile experiences which in themselves are in no way pathological, may, due to a present-day inhibition, become endowed with an excess of sexual energy. Once that has happened, they become urgent; being in conflict with adult psychic organization, they have to be kept down by repression. Thus, the chronic psychoneurosis with its infan-

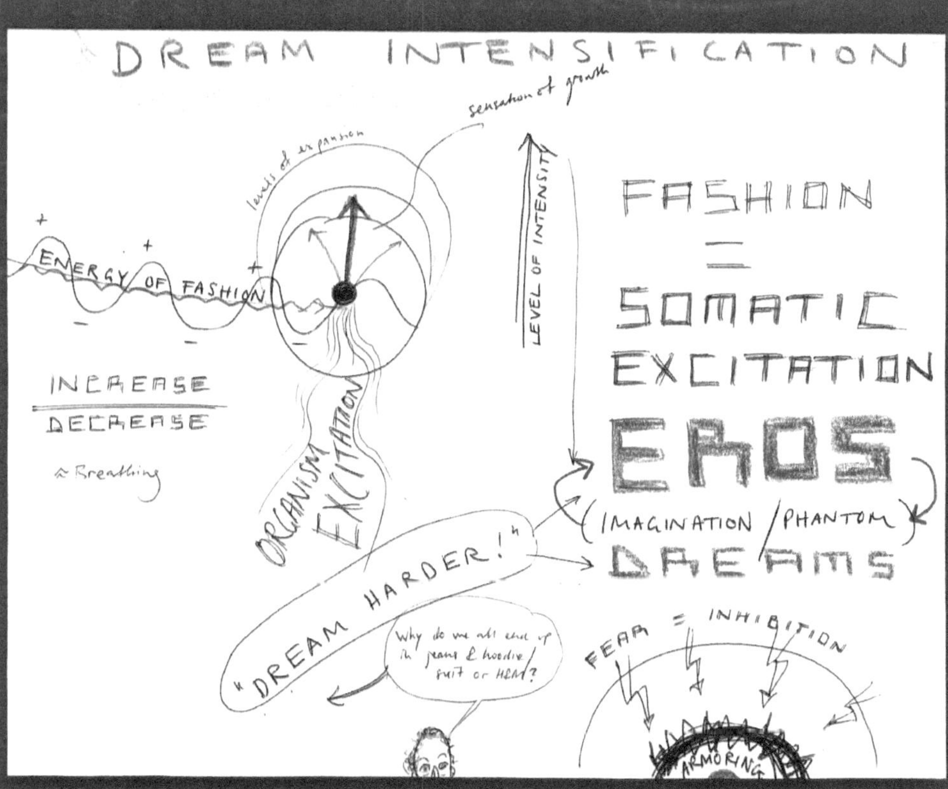

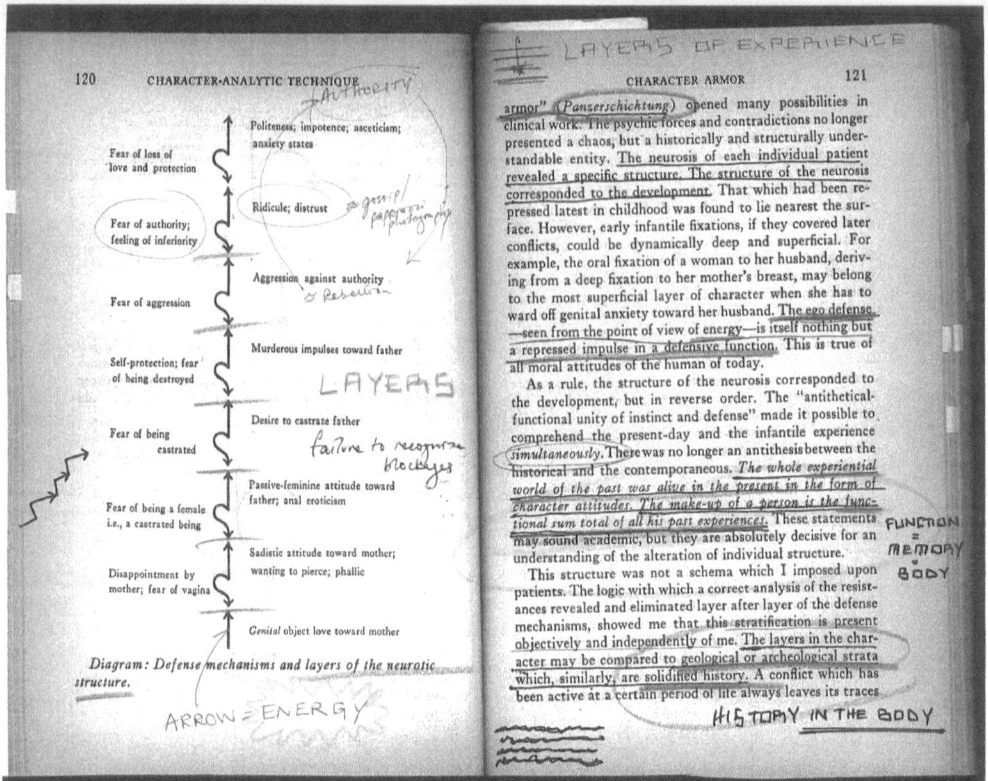

[handwritten: AUTHORITY]

Fear of loss of love and protection → Politeness; impotence; asceticism; anxiety states

Fear of authority; feeling of inferiority → Ridicule; distrust *[handwritten: = gossip / paparazzi photography]*

Fear of aggression → Aggression against authority *[handwritten: = Rebellion]*

Self-protection; fear of being destroyed → Murderous impulses toward father

[handwritten: LAYERS]

Fear of being castrated → Desire to castrate father *[handwritten: failure to recognize blockages]*

Fear of being a female i.e., a castrated being → Passive-feminine attitude toward father; anal eroticism

Disappointment by mother; fear of vagina → Sadistic attitude toward mother; wanting to pierce; phallic

Genital object love toward mother

Diagram: Defense mechanisms and layers of the neurotic structure.

[handwritten: ARROW = ENERGY]

[handwritten: LAYERS OF EXPERIENCE]

armor" (*Panzerschichtung*) opened many possibilities in clinical work. The psychic forces and contradictions no longer presented a chaos, but a historically and structurally understandable entity. The neurosis of each individual patient revealed a specific structure. The structure of the neurosis corresponded to the development. That which had been repressed latest in childhood was found to lie nearest the surface. However, early infantile fixations, if they covered later conflicts, could be dynamically deep and superficial. For example, the oral fixation of a woman to her husband, deriving from a deep fixation to her mother's breast, may belong to the most superficial layer of character when she has to ward off genital anxiety toward her husband. The ego defense—seen from the point of view of energy—is itself nothing but a repressed impulse in a defensive function. This is true of all moral attitudes of the human of today.

As a rule, the structure of the neurosis corresponded to the development, but in reverse order. The "antithetical-functional unity of instinct and defense" made it possible to comprehend the present-day and the infantile experience simultaneously. There was no longer an antithesis between the historical and the contemporaneous. *The whole experiential world of the past was alive in the present in the form of character attitudes. The make-up of a person is the functional sum total of all his past experiences.* These statements may sound academic, but they are absolutely decisive for an understanding of the alteration of individual structure.

This structure was not a schema which I imposed upon patients. The logic with which a correct analysis of the resistances revealed and eliminated layer after layer of the defense mechanisms, showed me that this stratification is present objectively and independently of me. The layers in the character may be compared to geological or archeological strata which, similarly, are solidified history. A conflict which has been active at a certain period of life always leaves its traces

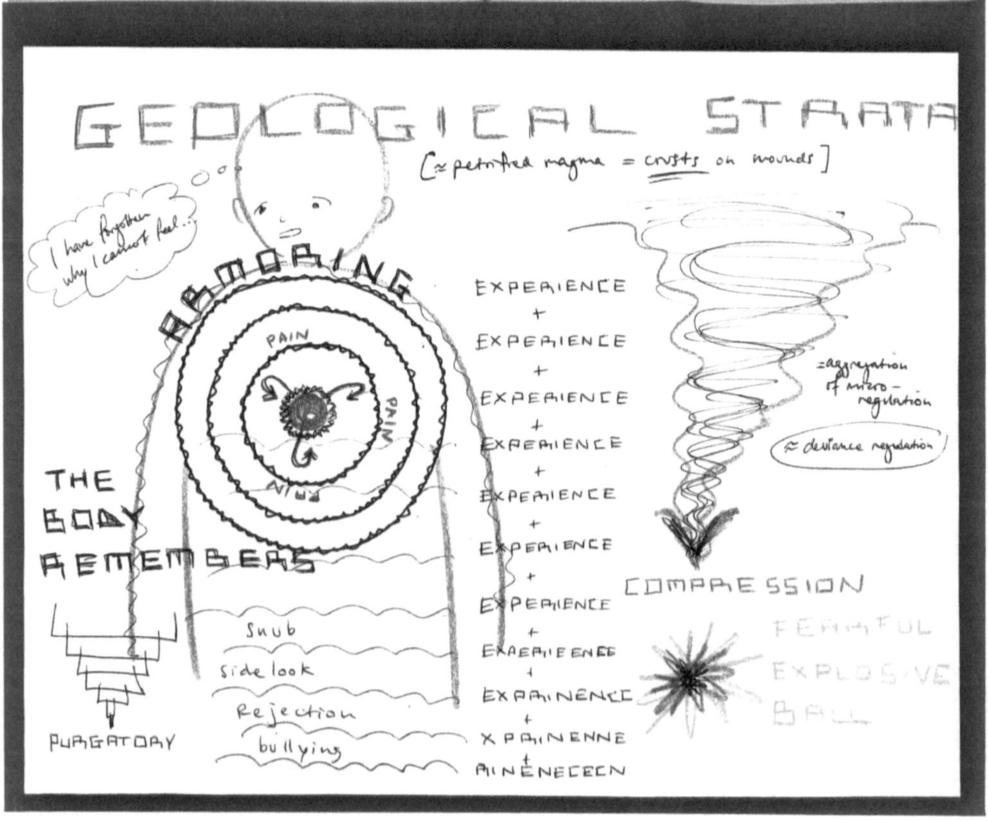

[handwritten: FUNCTION = MEMORY = BODY]

[handwritten: HISTORY IN THE BODY]

[handwritten notes and sketch]

GEOLOGICAL STRATA

[= petrified magma = crusts on wounds]

I have forgotten why I cannot feel…

ARMORING

PAIN

PAIN

PAIN

THE BODY REMEMBERS

PURGATORY

Snub

side look

Rejection

bullying

EXPERIENCE
+
EXPERIENCE
+
EXPERIENCE
+
EXPERIENCE
+
EXPERIENCE
+
EXPERIENCE
+
EXPERIENCE
+
EXPERIENCE
+
EXAERIEENEE
+
EXPAINENCE
+
XPAINENNE
+
AINENECECN

= aggregation of micro-regulation

≈ deviance regulation

COMPRESSION

FEARFUL EXPLOSIVE BALL

pressure, which in turn necessitates increased moral defense. It makes a natural circulation of energy in the organism impossible. Self-regulation withdraws the energy from a desire which cannot be satisfied by transferring the energy to other goals or partners. It consists in a steady alternation of tension and release of tension, as do all natural functions. The individual with a moral character structure performs his work without inward participation, as a result of the demands of a "Thou shalt" which is alien to the ego. The individual with a sex-economic character structure performs his work in unison with his sexual interests, out of the large reservoir of vital energy. The individual with a moral structure appears to follow the rigid laws of the moral world; in fact, he only adjusts outwardly and rebels inwardly. Thus he is exposed in the highest degree to an unconscious compulsive and impulsive antisociality. The healthy, self-regulated individual does not adjust himself to the irrational part of the world and insists on his natural rights. To the neurotic moralist, he appears sick and antisocial; in reality he is incapable of antisocial actions. He develops a *natural* self-assurance, based on sexual potency. The individual with a moral structure, without exception, is genitally weak and therefore under the constant necessity of compensating, i.e., of developing a false, rigid self-assurance. He tolerates sexual happiness in others poorly, because this arouses him, while he is at the same time incapable of enjoying it also. To him, the sexual act is essentially a demonstration of "potency". To the individual with a genital structure, sexuality is a pleasurable experience and nothing but that; work is joyous vital activity and achievement. To the morally structured individual, work is burdensome duty or only a means of making a living.

The character armor is also different in the two types. The individual with a moral structure has to develop an armor which is restrictive, dominating every action, functioning

Neurotic character   *Genital character*

Reactive work — Protest, escape; Sexuality; Sexual energy, inhibited, repressed; Sexual repression; Biological nucleus.

Sex-economic work — Work; Oscillation of biological energy; No sexual repression; Biological nucleus.

Reactive work

The achievement is mechanical, forced, devoid of vitality; it serves the purpose of deadening the sexual urge and is in acute conflict with it. Only small amounts of biological energy can be discharged in an interest in work. Work is essentially unpleasurable. Sexual phantasies are intense and interfere with work; thus, they have to be repressed, thereby creating neurotic mechanisms which in turn decrease the working capacity still further. The reduced achievement in work charges every sexual impulse with guilt feelings. Self-confidence is reduced; this leads to compensatory neurotic phantasies of grandeur.

Sex-economic work

Here, the biological energy oscillates between work and sexual activity. Work and sexual activity are not opposites; that is, work does not serve to suppress the sexual urge, nor are there any sexual phantasies to interfere with work. Rather, work and sexuality support each other on the basis of a sound self-confidence. The interest is concentrated, fully and without conflict, either in work or in sexual activity, borne by the feeling of potency and the capacity to give oneself.

Diagram: Reactive and sex-economic way of working.

automatically regardless of what the external situation may be. The attitude cannot be changed, even though he may try to change it. The moralistic bureaucrat remains so even in bed. The healthy character type, on the other hand, is able to close up in one place and to open up in another. He

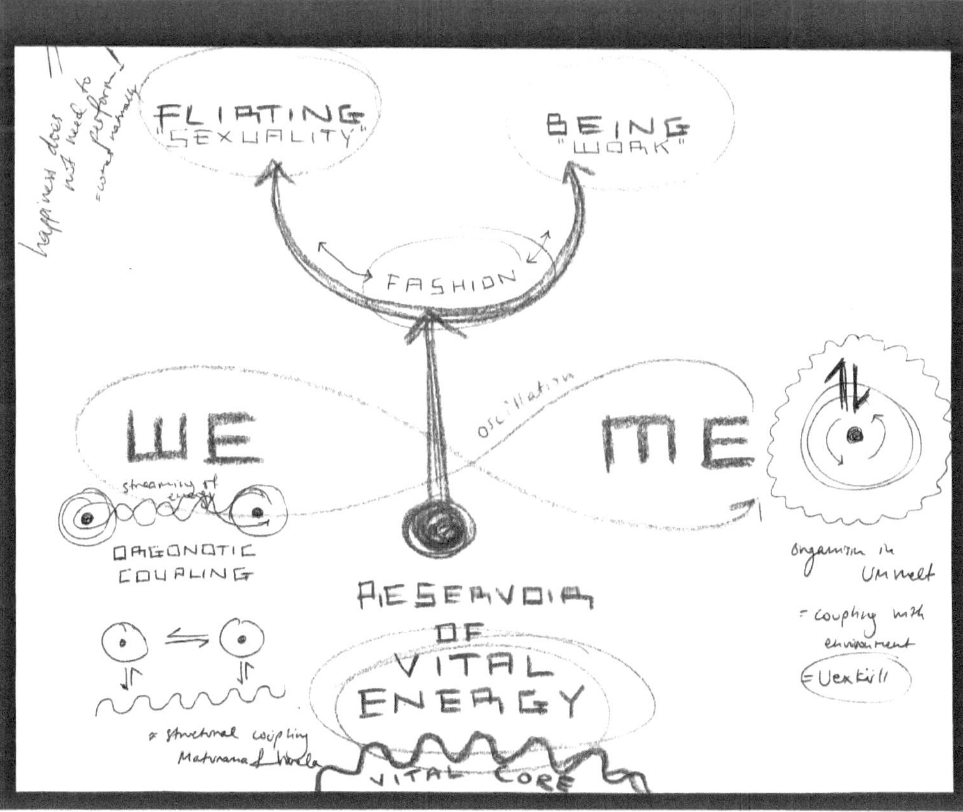

of justification for the lengths beyond this to which civilized society goes in actually denying the existence of these manifestations".

The formation of the sex-negative character structure, then, was the real, though unconscious, goal of education. Consequently, psychoanalytic pedagogy could no longer be discussed without discussing the problem of structure; neither could the latter be discussed without defining the *goal* of education. Education serves the purposes of the social order of any given time. If this social order contradicts the interest of the child, then education must leave the child out of consideration, and must do one of two things: either openly relinquish its set goal, "the welfare of the child", or else *pretend* to advocate it. This kind of education failed to distinguish between the *compulsive family* which suppresses the children, from the *family* which is built upon the deep natural love relationship between parents and children, and which is constantly being destroyed by the compulsive family relationships. Education, furthermore, failed to take cognizance of the gigantic revolution which had been taking place since the turn of the century in human sex life as well as in family life. With its "ideas" and "reforms" it was— and still is—hobbling far behind the actual changes. In short, it was caught in its own irrational motives of which it did not know nor dared to know.

Nevertheless, the plague of the neuroses is comparable to a pestilence. It disintegrates everything that human effort, thinking and work creates. Pestilence was attacked without hindrance, because such attack did not encroach either on profit or on mystical emotional interests. To fight against the plague of the neuroses is far more difficult. Everything that thrives on human mysticism clings to it and possesses power. Who would accept the argument that the psychic plague should not be attacked because the necessary measures of mental hygiene would be asking too much of the people?

Blaming it on lack of funds is a poor excuse. The sums that go up in smoke in one week of the war would be enough to provide for the hygienic needs of millions and millions. We are also apt to underestimate the gigantic forces that lie fallow in people and press towards expression and action.

Sex-economy had comprehended the biological goal of human striving, which was at variance with human *structure* and certain institutions of our social order. Freud sacrificed the goal of happiness to the existing human structure and the existing sexual chaos. There was nothing left for me to do but to retain the goal and to study the laws according to which this human structure *develops* and can be *altered*. I had no idea of the extent of the problem, let alone of the fact that neurotic psychic structure becomes *somatic innervation*, a "second nature", as it were.

For all his pessimism, Freud could not let matters rest in such a state of hopelessness. His final statement was:

"The fateful question of the human species seems to me to be whether and to what extent its cultural development will succeed in mastering the derangements of communal life caused by the human instinct of aggression and self-destruction. . . . And now it may be expected that the other of the two 'heavenly forces', eternal Eros, will put forth his strength so as to maintain himself against his equally immortal adversary".

This statement was much more than the turn of phrase for which it was taken by the psychoanalysts, certainly more than just a brilliant remark. *"Eros" presupposes full sexual capacity.* Full sexual capacity, in turn, presupposes a general affirmation of life, and a fostering of it on the part of society. Freud seemed secretly to wish me luck in my undertaking. He expressed himself obscurely, but the very material ways had indeed been found which would one day fulfill his hope: *Only the liberation of the natural capacity for love in human beings can master their sadistic destructiveness.*

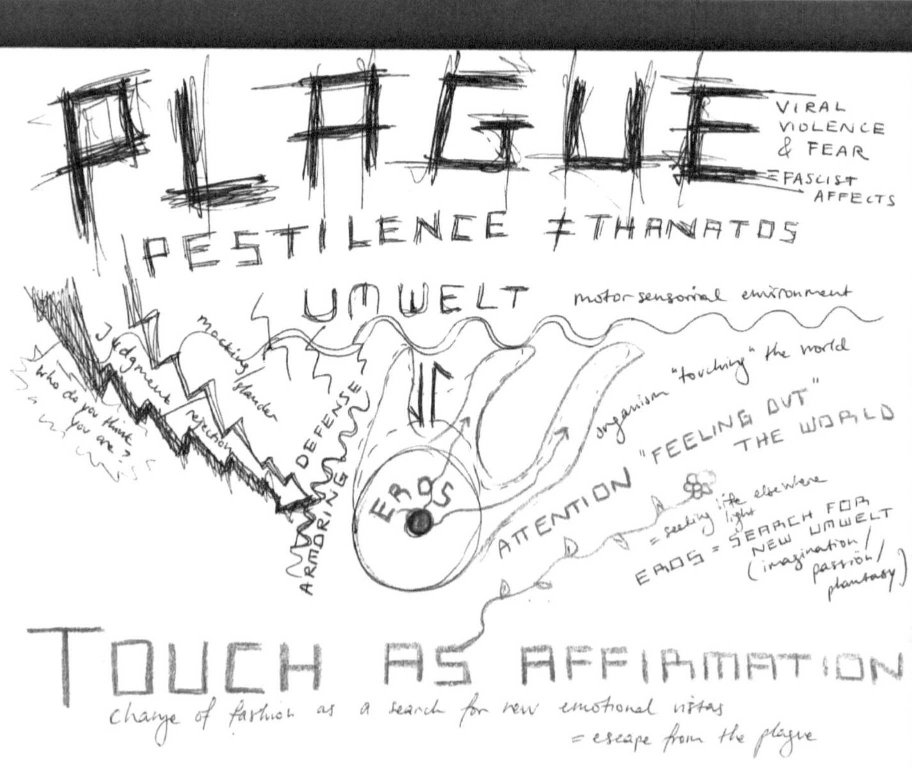

eyes knew: The masses of people *felt helpless and incapable of taking the responsibility for the solution of the chaotic social problems within the old political system and frame of thinking.* The Führer should and would do it *for them.*

Hitler promised the abolition of democratic discussion of opinion. The masses of people came running to him. They had long since grown tired of these discussions, because they had always evaded their personal everyday concerns, that is, that which was *subjectively* important. They did not want discussions of "the budget" or of "high diplomacy"; they wanted actual, true knowledge about their own lives. When they did not get that, they gave themselves over to authoritarian leadership and the illusionary protection which was promised to them.

Hitler promised the abolition of the freedom of the individual and the establishment of the *"freedom of the nation".* Enthusiastically, the masses of people exchanged their potentialities for individual freedom for *illusionary* freedom, that is, freedom through identification with an idea; they did so because this illusionary freedom relieved them of any individual *responsibility.* They craved *a "freedom" which the Führer should conquer for them and guarantee to them:* the freedom to howl, to escape from the truth into a fundamental falsehood, to be sadistic, to brag—though one was in actuality a cipher—about one's superior race, to impress girls with uniforms instead of strong human qualities, to sacrifice oneself for imperialistic goals instead of the actual struggles of everyday life, etc., etc.

The previous education of the masses of people towards the recognition of a formal, political authority instead of an authority based on *factual* knowledge formed the soil in which the Fascist demand for authority could readily strike roots. Fascism, therefore, was not a new kind of philosophy, as its friends and many of its enemies wanted us to believe; much less even does it have anything to do with a rational

revolution against intolerable social conditions; Fascism is nothing but *the extreme reactionary consequence of all undemocratic types of leadership of the past.* Neither is the *race theory* anything new; it is nothing but the consistently and brutally applied *continuation of the old theories of heredity and degeneration.* It is for this reason that the psychiatrists of the hereditarian school and the eugenicists of the old school were particularly accessible to Fascism.

What is new in the Fascist movement is the fact that the extreme political reaction succeeded in making use of the deep longings of the masses of people for freedom. *Intense longing for freedom plus fear of the responsibility of freedom results in Fascist mentality,* no matter whether it is found in a Fascist or a Democrat.

What is new in Fascism is that *the masses of people themselves assented to their own subjugation and actively brought it about.* The craving for authority proved stronger than the wish for independence.

Hitler promised the subjugation of woman to man, the abolition of her economic independence, her exclusion from the process of determining social life, and her relegation to the home and hearth. The women, whose individual freedom had been suppressed for centuries and who had developed the fear of an independent way of living in a particularly high degree, were the first to hail him.

Hitler promised the abolition of socialist and democratic organizations. The socialist and democratic masses hastened to him because their organizations, though they had done a great deal of talking about freedom, had not as much as mentioned the difficult problem of human craving for authority and their helplessness in matters of practical politics. The masses of people were disillusioned by the irresolute attitude of the old democratic institutions. *Disillusionment in the liberal organizations plus economic crisis plus tremendous urge for freedom result in Fascist mentality,* that is, in the

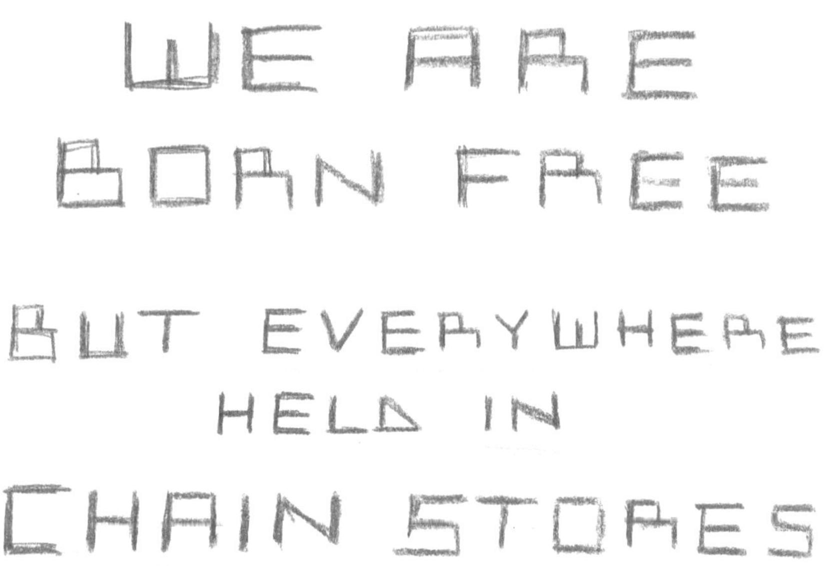

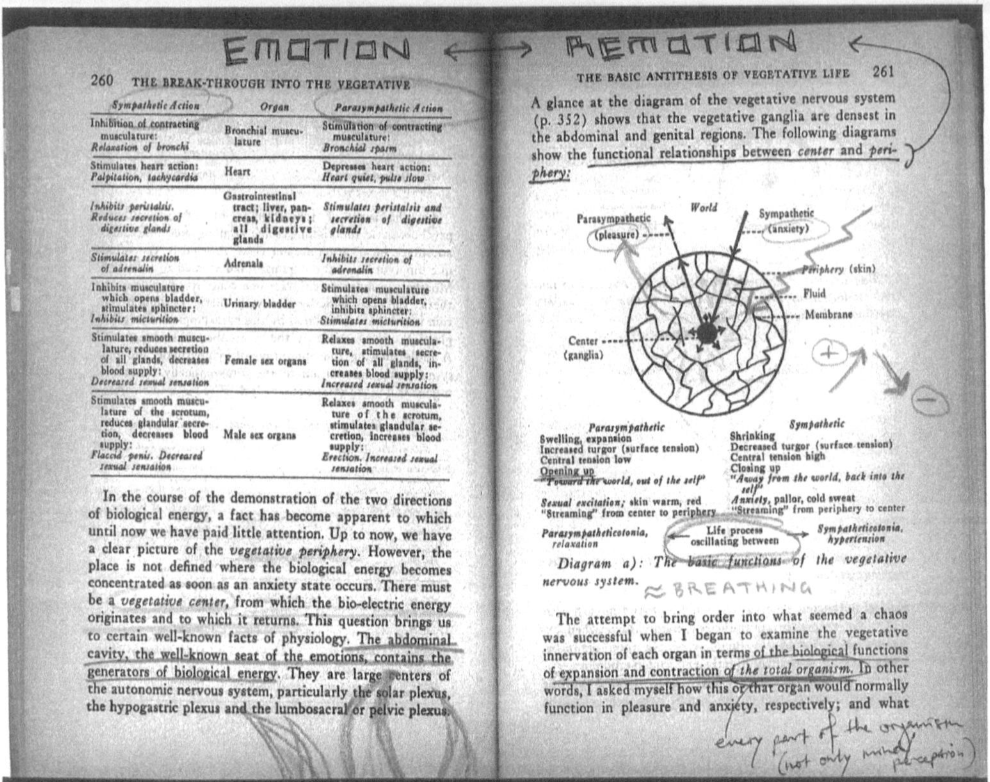

Sympathetic Action	Organ	Parasympathetic Action
Inhibition of contracting musculature: *Relaxation of bronchi*	Bronchial musculature	Stimulation of contracting musculature: *Bronchial spasm*
Stimulates heart action: *Palpitation, tachycardia*	Heart	Depresses heart action: *Heart quiet, pulse slow*
Inhibits peristalsis. Reduces secretion of digestive glands	Gastrointestinal tract; liver, pancreas, kidneys; all digestive glands	Stimulates peristalsis and secretion of digestive glands
Stimulates secretion of adrenalin	Adrenals	Inhibits secretion of adrenalin
Inhibits musculature which opens bladder, stimulates sphincter: *Inhibits micturition*	Urinary bladder	Stimulates musculature which opens bladder, inhibits sphincter: *Stimulates micturition*
Stimulates smooth musculature, reduces secretion of all glands, decreases blood supply: *Decreased sexual sensation*	Female sex organs	Relaxes smooth musculature, stimulates secretion of all glands, increases blood supply: *Increased sexual sensation*
Stimulates smooth musculature of the scrotum, reduces glandular secretion, decreases blood supply: *Flaccid penis. Decreased sexual sensation*	Male sex organs	Relaxes smooth musculature of the scrotum, stimulates glandular secretion, increases blood supply: *Erection. Increased sexual sensation*

In the course of the demonstration of the two directions of biological energy, a fact has become apparent to which until now we have paid little attention. Up to now, we have a clear picture of the *vegetative periphery*. However, the place is not defined where the biological energy becomes concentrated as soon as an anxiety state occurs. There must be a *vegetative center*, from which the bio-electric energy originates and to which it returns. This question brings us to certain well-known facts of physiology. The abdominal cavity, the well-known seat of the emotions, contains the generators of biological energy. They are large centers of the autonomic nervous system, particularly the solar plexus, the hypogastric plexus and the lumbosacral or pelvic plexus.

A glance at the diagram of the vegetative nervous system (p. 352) shows that the vegetative ganglia are densest in the abdominal and genital regions. The following diagrams show the functional relationships between *center* and *periphery*:

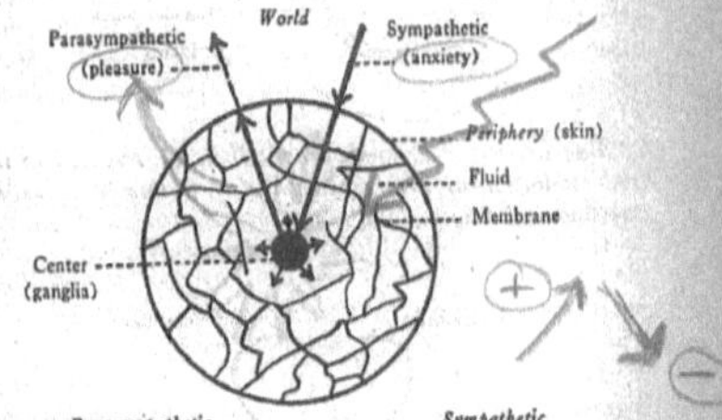

Parasympathetic
Swelling, expansion
Increased turgor (surface tension)
Central tension low
Opening up
"*Toward the world, out of the self*"
Sexual excitation; skin warm, red
"Streaming" from center to periphery
Parasympatheticotonia, relaxation

Sympathetic
Shrinking
Decreased turgor (surface tension)
Central tension high
Closing up
"*Away from the world, back into the self*"
Anxiety, pallor, cold sweat
"Streaming" from periphery to center
Sympatheticotonia, hypertension

Life process oscillating between

Diagram a): The basic functions of the vegetative nervous system.

≈ BREATHING

The attempt to bring order into what seemed a chaos was successful when I began to examine the vegetative innervation of each organ in terms of the biological functions of expansion and contraction of *the total organism*. In other words, I asked myself how this or that organ would normally function in pleasure and anxiety, respectively; and what

every part of the organism (not only mind/perception)

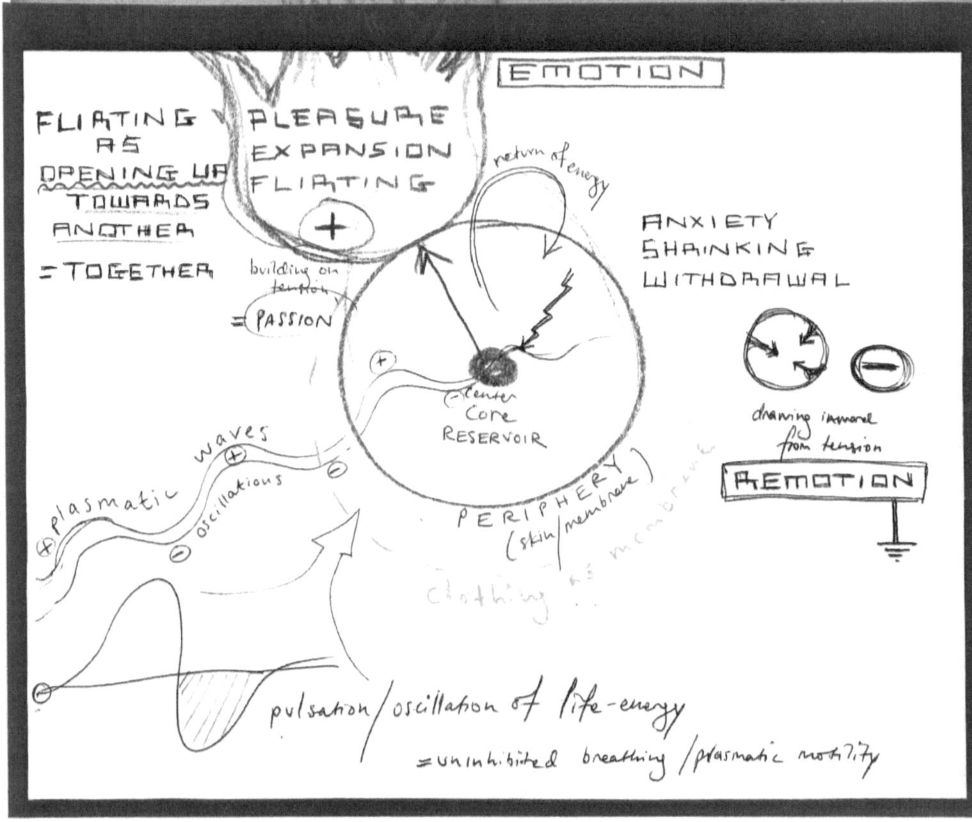

EMOTION

FLIRTING AS OPENING UP TOWARDS ANOTHER = TOGETHER

PLEASURE EXPANSION FLIRTING

+

building on tension = PASSION

return of energy

ANXIETY SHRINKING WITHDRAWAL

Center Core RESERVOIR

plasmatic waves

oscillations

PERIPHERY (skin/membrane)

clothing as membrane

drawing inward from tension

REMOTION

pulsation/oscillation of life-energy = uninhibited breathing/plasmatic motility pendulum-like, between parasympathetic expansion (expiration) and sympathetic contraction (inspiration). In formulating these theoretical considerations, I had in mind the rhythmic behavior of an ameba, a medusa or a heart. The function of respiration is too complicated to be briefly presented here in terms of these new insights.

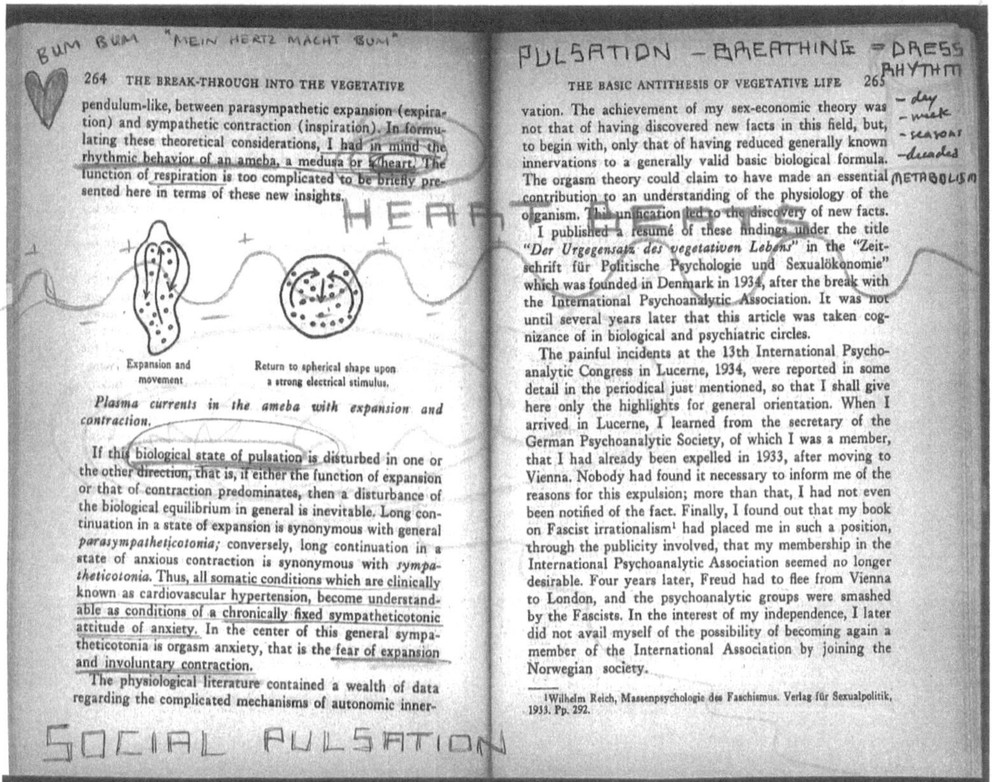

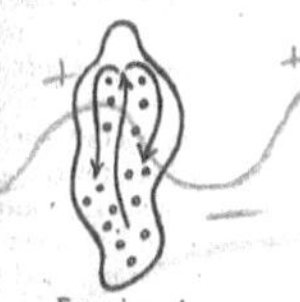

Plasma currents in the ameba with expansion and contraction.

If this biological state of pulsation is disturbed in one or the other direction, that is, if either the function of expansion or that of contraction predominates, then a disturbance of the biological equilibrium in general is inevitable. Long continuation in a state of expansion is synonymous with general *parasympatheticotonia;* conversely, long continuation in a state of anxious contraction is synonymous with *sympatheticotonia.* Thus, all somatic conditions which are clinically known as cardiovascular hypertension, become understandable as conditions of a chronically fixed sympatheticotonic attitude of anxiety. In the center of this general sympatheticotonia is orgasm anxiety, that is the fear of expansion and involuntary contraction.

The physiological literature contained a wealth of data regarding the complicated mechanisms of autonomic inner-

vation. The achievement of my sex-economic theory was not that of having discovered new facts in this field, but, to begin with, only that of having reduced generally known innervations to a generally valid basic biological formula. The orgasm theory could claim to have made an essential contribution to an understanding of the physiology of the organism. This unification led to the discovery of new facts.

I published a resumé of these findings under the title *"Der Urgegensatz des vegetativen Lebens"* in the "Zeitschrift für Politische Psychologie und Sexualökonomie" which was founded in Denmark in 1934, after the break with the International Psychoanalytic Association. It was not until several years later that this article was taken cognizance of in biological and psychiatric circles.

The painful incidents at the 13th International Psychoanalytic Congress in Lucerne, 1934, were reported in some detail in the periodical just mentioned, so that I shall give here only the highlights for general orientation. When I arrived in Lucerne, I learned from the secretary of the German Psychoanalytic Society, of which I was a member, that I had already been expelled in 1933, after moving to Vienna. Nobody had found it necessary to inform me of the reasons for this expulsion; more than that, I had not even been notified of the fact. Finally, I found out that my book on Fascist irrationalism[1] had placed me in such a position, through the publicity involved, that my membership in the International Psychoanalytic Association seemed no longer desirable. Four years later, Freud had to flee from Vienna to London, and the psychoanalytic groups were smashed by the Fascists. In the interest of my independence, I later did not avail myself of the possibility of becoming again a member of the International Association by joining the Norwegian society.

[1] Wilhelm Reich, Massenpsychologie des Faschismus. Verlag für Sexualpolitik, 1933. Pp. 292.

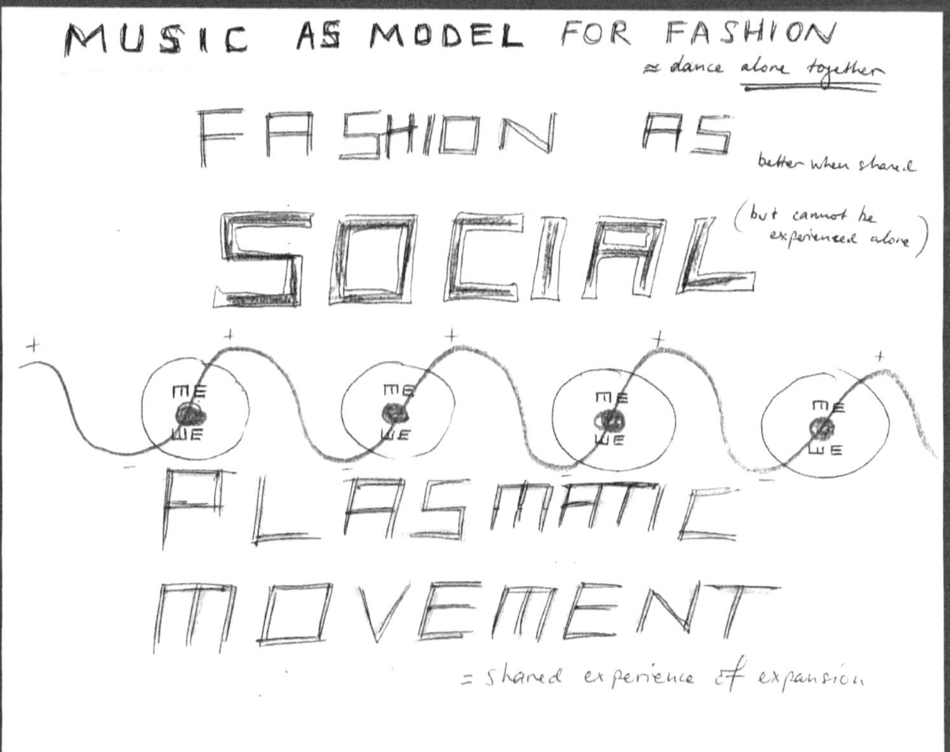

quires bio-electrical charge. *Orgastic gratification is a bio-electrical discharge, followed by a mechanical relaxation* (detumescence).

The biological process of expansion, as exemplified in the erection of an organ or the putting out of peudopodia in the ameba, *is the outward manifestation of the movement of bio-electric energy from the center to the periphery of the organism*. What is moving here is—in the psychic as well as the somatic sense—the bio-electrical charge itself.

Since only vegetative pleasure sensations are accompanied by an increased charge of the body surface, *pleasurable excitation must be considered the specifically productive process in the biological system*. All other affects, such as pain, annoyance, anxiety, depression, as well as pressure, are antithetical to it from the point of view of energy, and consequently represent functions negative to life. Thus, *the process of sexual pleasure is the life process* per se. This is not just a manner of speaking, but an experimentally proven fact.

Anxiety, as the fundamental functional antithesis of sexuality, is concurrent with death. It is, however, not identical with death. For, in death the central source of energy becomes extinguished; in anxiety, however, the energy is withdrawn from the periphery and dammed up in the center, creating the subjective sensation of oppression (*angustiae*).

These facts give the concept of sex-economy a concrete meaning in terms of natural science. It means *the manner of regulation of bio-electric energy*, or, what is the same thing, of *the economy of the sexual energies of the individual*. "Sex-economy" means the manner in which an individual handles his bio-electric energy; how much of it he dams up and how much of it he discharges orgastically. As we have to take the bio-electric energy of the organism as our basic point of departure, a new avenue of approach to the understanding of organic disease is opened.

The neuroses now appear to us in a fundamentally different light than to the psychoanalysts. They are by no means just the result of unresolved psychic conflicts and infantile fixations. *Rather, these fixations and conflicts cause fundamental disturbances of the economy of the bio-electrical energy and thus become anchored somatically*. For this reason, a separation of psychic from somatic processes is not possible or tenable. Psychic illnesses are biological disturbances, manifesting themselves in the somatic as well as in the psychic sphere. The basis of the disturbances is a deviation from the natural modes of discharge of biological energy.

Psyche and soma form a functional unity, having at the same time an antithetical relationship. Both function on the basis of biological laws. Deviation from these biological laws is a result of social factors in the environment. *The psychosomatic structure is the result of a clash between social and biological functions.*

The function of the orgasm becomes the measuring rod of psychophysical functioning because in it the function of biological energy is expressed.

2. THE THEORETICAL SOLUTION OF THE CONFLICT BETWEEN MECHANISM AND VITALISM

When it was found that the formula of tension and charge applied to all involuntary functions of living substance, the question suggested itself as to whether it also applies to processes occurring in inanimate nature. Neither the literature nor discussions with physicists revealed the existence of an inorganic function in which a mechanical tension (through filling up with fluid) would lead to an electric charge, and then to an electric discharge and mechanical relaxation (through evacuation of fluid). It is true that in

N 219   Psychology $2.95
SBN 374.5.0204.8

THE DISCOVERY OF THE ORGONE

The Function of the Orgasm

by WILHELM REICH, M.D.

This book summarizes Wilhelm Reich's medical and scientific work with the human organism over a period of twenty years, and it presents the whole development of this work in its rapid progression from the realm of psychology into that of biology.

The discovery of the orgone was the result of a consistent clinical investigation of the concept of "psychic energy," at first in the realm of psychiatry. Experience has shown beyond any doubt that the knowledge of the *emotional* functions of the biological energy is indispensable for the understanding of its *physiological* and *physical* functions. The biological emotions which govern the psychic processes are in themselves the immediate expression of a strictly physical energy, the cosmic orgone.

THE NOONDAY PRESS

19 Union Square West   New York 10003

Where do you feel fashion?

- extra heartbeat?
- sweaty palms?
- stress?
- arousal?

Place your emotions on the figure

Type of emotion:

Where in body:

What garment:

Situation:

Type of emotion:

Where in body:

What garment:

Situation:

Type of emotion:

Where in body:

What garment:

Situation:

Type of emotion:

Where in body:

What garment:

Situation:

Type of emotion:

Where in body:

What garment:

Situation:

Type of emotion:

Where in body:

What garment:

Situation:

Rationale:

Following Reich's studies on the bioelectric currents of the body, we could think of fashion as an emotion in the body, measured by observing our autonomic nervous system. What is "fashionable" is not what some icon or the media point to, but what gets our energies going. But how are we to map or trace the experience of fashion in the body?

[Disclaimer: The artist recognizes that these experiments are his own, and that they do not in any way represent Reich's experimental work.]

With whom do you experience fashion?

- at the nighclub?
- at a reunion?
- on the subway?
- at the internship?

Map the context of your emotions

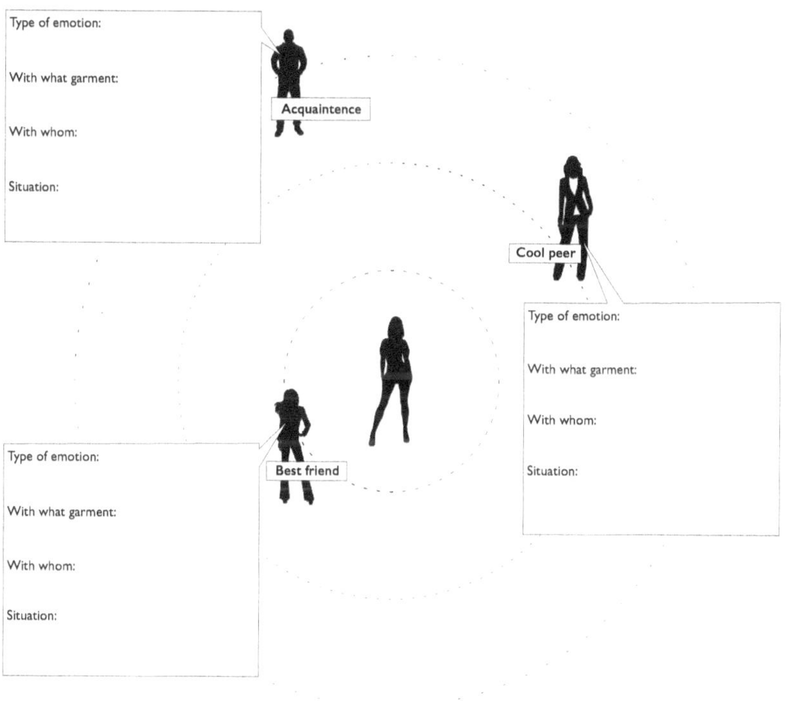

Rationale:

Fashion cannot be experienced in solitude. It is biosocial pulsation attracting and connecting people, and is thus situated in socio-political context. As a social dynamic, we need to map out in what social, spatial, and temporal contexts fashion works. Recall when your closest friend or acquaintence made a comment on your clothes; what did it feel like?

Who do you follow?
Who do you lead?

Place yourself in the social hierarchies

Following: Fashion

Inspiration:

Why:

Following: Media

Inspiration:

Why:

Leading: Fashion

They imitate me:

How does it feel?

Leading: Media

They follow me:

How does it feel?

Rationale:

A basic paradox in life, emphasized by Reich, is that we are born free, but everywhere behave like slaves: people are not "fooled" by leaders, but desire to be led. Fashion is not different; we are free to dress however we like, yet we crave leaders to tell us what is right. We seek inspiration, people to imitate and emulate. We crave leaders and to become followers, and people may in turn follow us. Who follows who?

[Disclaimer: The artist recognizes that these experiments are his own, and that they do not in any way represent Reich's experimental work.]

How do your garments' excitement levels change over time?

Compare two garments

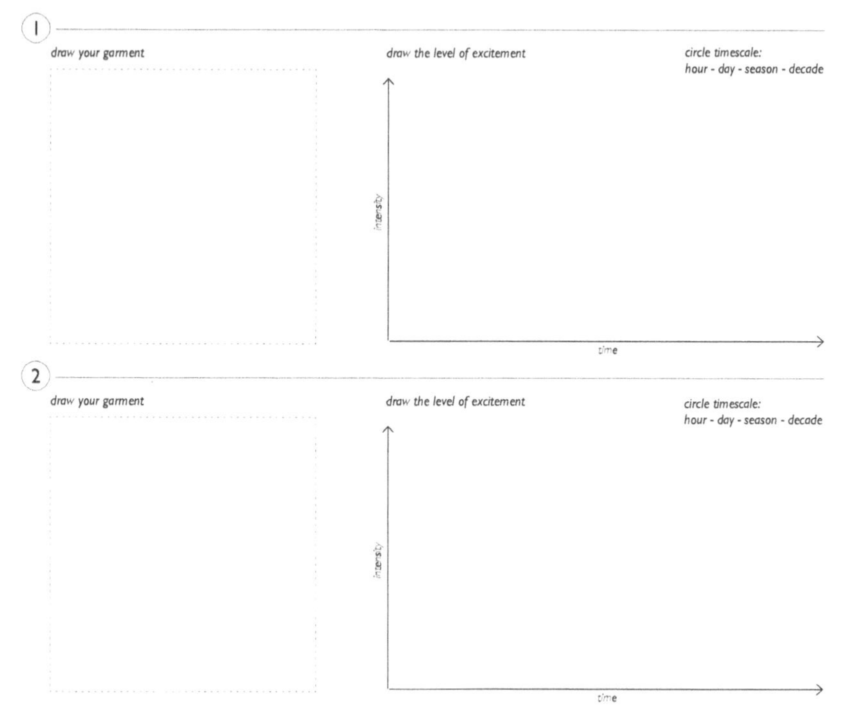

Rationale:

Fashion is not merely image or material, but an energetic charge that powers our entire organism and living environment. Perhaps such intensity could be somewhat related to Reich's orgone energy. Certain garments excite and amplify our shared energies better than others. What actions and processes animates your garments? What situations change their charge? Record your observations.

[Disclaimer: The artist recognizes that these experiments are his own, and that they do not in any way represent Reich's experimental work.]

REFERENCES

Ackerman, Diane (1990) *A natural history of the senses*, New York: Vintage Books.

Ahmed, Sara (2015) *The cultural politics of emotion*, New York: Routledge.

Aron, Arthur & Elaine Aron (1986) *Love and the expansion of self: Understanding attraction and satisfaction.* New York: Harper & Row.

Bancroft, Alison (2012) *Fashion and psychoanalysis: Styling the self,* London: I.B.Tauris.

Barthes, Roland (1983) *The fashion system,* New York, NY: Hill and Wang.

Barnard, Malcolm (1996) *Fashion as communication,* London: Routledge.

Barrett, Lisa Feldman (2017) *How emotions are made: the secret life of the brain,* London: Macmillan.

Bataille, Georges (1991) *The accursed share: an essay on general economy,* New York: Zone.

Baudrillard, Jean (1996) *The system of objects,* Verso, New York.

Bauman, Zygmunt (2006) *Liquid fear,* Cambridge: Polity Press.

Bauman, Zygmunt (2007) *Consuming life,* London: Polity.

Bauman, Zygmunt (2010) "Perpetuum mobile," *Critical studies in fashion & Beauty* 1.1 (2010): 55-63.

Becker, Ernest (1973) *The denial of death,* New York: Free Press.

Becker, Ernest (1975) *Escape from evil,* New York: Free Press.

Beckman, Frida (2013) *Between desire and pleasure: A deleuzian theory of sexuality,* Edinburgh: Edinburg University Press.

Ben-Ze'ev, Aaron (2000) *The subtlety of emotions,* Cambridge: MIT Press

Bennett, Jane (2004) "The force of things steps toward an ecology of matter." *Political theory,* 32.3, pp. 347-372.

Bennett, Jane (2010) *Vibrant matter: a political ecology of things,* Durham: Duke University Press.

Bennett, Philip (2010) "Wilhelm Reich's early writings on work democracy: A theoretical basis for challenging fascism then and now," *Capitalism Nature Socialism*, Vol 21, Iss 1: pp. 53-73.

Berardi, Franco (2009) *The soul at work: From alienation to autonomy*, Los Angeles: Semiotext(e).

Bissinger, Buzz (2013) "My Gucci addiction," GQ *magazine*, April 2013,.

Blackman, Lisa (2012) *Immaterial bodies: affect, embodiment, mediation*, London: Sage.

Bourdieu, Pierre (1984) *Distinction: A social critique of the judgment of taste*, London: Routledge.

de Botton, Alain (2012) *How to think more about sex*, London: Macmillan.

de Botton, Alain (n.d.) "Why flirtig matters," *The book of life*, http://www.thebookoflife.org/why-flirting-matters/

Braidotti, Rosi (2000) "Teratologies", Buchanan & Colebrook (eds) *Deleuze and feminist theory*, Edinburgh: Edinburgh University press pp. 156-172.

Braidotti, Rosi (2002) *Metamorphoses: Towards a materialist theory of becoming*, Cambridge: Polity.

Braidotti, Rosi (2006) *Transpositions: On nomadic ethics*, Cambridge: Polity.

Brentari, Carlo (2015) *Jakob von Uexkull: The discovery of the Umwelt between biosemiotics and theoretical biology*, Dordrecht: Springer.

Brier, Soren (2008) *Cybersemiotics: Why information is not enough!*. Toronto: University of Toronto Press.

Brodie, Richard (1996) *Virus of the mind, the new science of the meme*, Seattle: Integral Press

von Busch, Otto (2014) "'a suit, of his own earning': Fashion supremacy and sustainable fashion activism", in Fletcher & Tham (eds) *The Routledge handbook of sustainability and fashion*, London: Routledge.

Buss, David (1994) *The evolution of desire: Strategies of human mating*, New York: Basic Books.

Buss, David (2000) *The dangerous passion: Why jealousy is as necessary as love and sex*, New York: Free Press.

Capra, Fritjof (1996) *The web of life*, New York: Anchor Books

Capra, Fritjof (2003) Interview by Jennifer Leonard, *Massive Change Radio*, October 28, 2003.

Cho, Gilsoo, Casali, John Casali & Eunjou Yi (2001) "Effect of fabric sound and touch on human subjective sensation", *Fibers and Polymers*, Vol.2, No.4, 196-202.

Clough, Patricia (2010) "The affective turn: Political economy, biomedia and bodies," in Gregg and Seigworth (eds) *The affect theory reader*, Durham: Duke University Press.

Corrington, Robert (2003) *Wilhelm Reich: Psychoanalyst and radical naturalist*, New York: Farrar, Straus and Giroux.

Crary, Jonathan (2013) *24/7: Late capitalism and the ends of sleep*, New York: Verso.

Dawkins, Richard (1976) *The selfish gene*, Oxford: Oxford University Press

Dawkins, Richard (1982) *The extended phenotype: the gene as the unit of selection*, Oxford: Freeman.

Deely, John (1986) "Semiotics as framework and direction" in John Deely, Brooke Willians and Felicia Kruse (eds) *Frontiers of semiotics*, Bloomington: Indiana University Press.

Deleuze, Gilles (1977) "Three group problems." *Semiotext(e)*, 2(3): pp. 99–109.

Deleuze, Gilles (1988) *Foucault*, London: Athlone.

Deleuze, Gilles (2001) "Dualism, monism and multiplicities (Desire-pleasure-jouissance)", *Contretemps 2*, May.

Deleuze, Gilles and Felix Guattari (1983) *Anti-Oedipus*, Minneapolis: University of Minnesota Press.

Deleuze, Gilles and Felix Guattari (1987) *A thousand plateaus*, Minneapolis: University of Minnesota Press.

Derrida, Jaqcues (2005) *Rogues: Two essays on reason*, Stanford: Stanford University Press

Eisenberger, Naomi I., Matthew D. Lieberman, and Kipling D. Williams (2003) "Does rejection hurt? An fMRI study of social exclusion." *Science* 302.5643: pp. 290-292.

Faris, Robert (2012) "Aggression, exclusivity, and status attainment in interpersonal networks." *Social Forces* 90(4), pp.1207-1235.

Featherstone, Mike (2010) "Body, image and affect in consumer culture," *Body & Society*, 16 (1): 193-221.

Fisher, Helen (2004) *Why we love: The nature and chemistry of romantic love*, New York: Henry Holt.

Fisher, Mark (2014) *Ghosts of my life: writings on depression, hauntology and lost futures*, Winchester: Zero Books

Fiske, Susan (2011) *Envy up, scorn down: how status divides us*, New York: Russell Sage Foundation.

Florkin, Marcel (1974) "Concepts of molecular biosemiotics and of molecular evolution." In Marcel Florkin & Elmer Stotz (eds) *Comprehensive Biochemistry*, vol29, part A, Amsterdam: Elsevier, pp. 1-124.

Flugel, John (1950) *The psychology of clothes*, London: Hogarth.

Fox, Nick and Pam Alldred (2017) *Sociology and the new materialism: theory, research, action*, Los Angeles: SAGE.

Freud, Sigmund (1938) "Three contributions to the theory of sex," in A.A. Brill (ed) (1938) *The basic writings of Sigmund Freud*, New York: Random House.

Freud, Sigmund (1962) *Civilization and its discontent*, New York: WW Norton.

Fromm, Erich (1957) *The art of loving*, London: Allen & Unwin.

Fuller, Robert (2008) *Spirituality in the flesh: Bodily sources of religious experience*, Oxford: Oxford University Press.

Giddens, Anthony (1992) *The transformation of intimacy*, Stanford: Stanford University Press.

Girard, René (1965) *Desire, deceit, and the novel*, Baltimore: Johns Hopkins University Press

Gregg, Melissa & Gregory Seigworth (eds) *The affect theory reader*, Durham: Duke University Press.

Griggin, Roger (2007) *Modernism and fascism: The sense of a beginning under Mussolini and Hitler*, Basingstoke: Palgrave.

Grosz, Elisabeth (2008), *Chaos, territory, art: Deleuze and the framing of the earth*, New York: Columbia University Press.

Guattari, Felix (1977 [1973]) "Everybody wants to be a fascist," *Semiotext(e)*, 2(3), pp. 87-98.

Guattari, Felix (1995) *Chaosmosis*, Indianapolis: Indiana University Press.

Han, Byung-Chul (2015) *The burnout society*, Stanford: Stanford University Press.

Han, Byung-Chul (2015b) *The transparency society*, Stanford: Stanford University Press.

Han, Byung-Chul (2017) *Psychopolitics: Neoliberalism and new technologies of power*. London: Verso.

Heller, Michael (2012) *Body psychotherapy: History, concepts, methods*, New York: WW Norton

Herz, John (1951) *Political realism and political idealism*, Chicago: University of Chicago Press

Herzog, Dagmar (2016) "Desire's politics: Felix Guattari and the renewal of the psychoanalytic left," *Psychoanalysis and History*, 18(1): pp. 7–37

Hird, Myra (2010) "Meeting with the microcosmos," *Environment and Planning D: Space and Society*, 28: 36-39.

Hollander, Anne (1978) *Seeing through clothes*, New York: Viking.

Illich, Ivan (1971) *Deschooling society*, New York: Harper & Row.

Izard, Carol & Brian Ackerman (2000) "Motivational, organizational, and regulatory functions of discrete emotions," in Lewis & Haviland-Jones (eds.) *Handboook of Emotions*, pp. 253-322.

James, Willam (1890) *The principles of psychology*, Vol. 1, New York: Henry Holt.

Jonas, Hans (1992) "The burden and blessing of mortality," *The Hastings Center Report*, Vol. 22, No. 1 (Jan. - Feb., 1992), pp. 34-40.

Kaiser, Susan (2013) *Fashion and cultural studies*, London: Bloomsbury.

König, Rene (1973) *The restless image: A sociology of fashion*. London: Allen & Unwind.

Lagerfeld, Karl (2007) *Lagerfeld confidential*, documentary by Rodolphe Marconi.

Laver, James (1969) *Modesty in dress: An inquiry into the fundamentals of fashion*, Boston: Houghton Mifflin.

Lawlor,Leonard (2006) *The implications of immanence: Toward a new concept of life*, New York: Fordham University Press.

Lee, Michele (2003) *Fashion victim: Our love-hate relationship with dressing, shopping, and the cost of style*, New York: Broadway Books.

Lepinay, Vincent-Antonin (2007) "Economy of the germ: Capital, accumulation and vibration" *Economy and Society*, Vol. 36, No. 4.

Lipovetsky, Gilles (1994) *The empire of fashion: dressing modern democracy*, Princeton: Princeton University Press.

Lurie, Alison (1981) *The language of clothes*, New York: Random House.

Margulis, Lynn (1998) *The symbiotic planet: A new look at evolution*, London: Weidenfeld & Nicolson

Margulis, Lynn & Dorian Sagan (1986) *Origins of sex: Three billion years of genetic recombination*, New Haven: Yale University Press.

Massumi, Brian (2002) *Parables for the virtual: Movement, affect, sensation*, Durham: Duke University Press.

Maturana, Humberto (1980) "Biology of cognition" in Maturana & Varela (eds) *Autopoiesis and cognition: The realization of the living*, Dordrecht: Reidel.

Maturana, Humberto (1988) "Reality: The search for objectivity or the quest for a compelling argument", *Irish Journal of Psychology*, available at http://www.univie.ac.at/constructivism/papers/maturana/88-reality.html

Maturana, Humberto (1997) "Metadesign" in Brouwer, Joke & Hoekendijk, Carla (eds) *TechnoMorphica*, Rotterdam: V2.

Maturana, Humberto (2002) "Autopoiesis, structural coupling and cognition: A history of these and other notions in the biology of cognition," *Cybernetics & Human Knowing*, 9(3/4), 5-34.

Maturana, Humberto & Francisco Varela (1992) *The tree of knowledge: The biological roots of human understanding.* Boston: Shambhala.

Mearsheimer, John (2001) *The tragedy of great power politics,* New York: Norton.

Merleau-Ponty, Maurice (1968) *The visible and the invisible,* Evanston: Northwestern University Press.

Miller, Joshua (2005) "Fashion and democratic relationships," *Polity,* Vol. 37, No. 1, pp. 3-23

Mogensen, Preben (1992) "Towards a provotyping approach in systems development", *Scandinavian journal of information systems,* Vol. 4.

Morgenthau, Hans (1946) *Scientific man vs. power politics,* London: Latimer House.

Nancy, Jean-Luc & Adele van Reeth (2017) *Coming,* New York: Fordham University Press

Orenstein, Peggy (2016) *Girls & sex: Navigating the complicated new landscape,* London: Oneworld.

Pagold, Suzanne (2000) *De långas sammansvärjning,* Stockholm: Bonniers.

Parisi, Luciana (2004) *Abstract sex: Philosophy, bio-technology, and the mutations of desire,* London: Continuum.

Plutchik, Robert (2003) *Emotions and life: Perspectives from psychology, biology, and evolution,* Washington DC: American Psychological Association.

Polan, Brenda & Roger Tredre (2009) *The great fashion designers,* Oxford: Berg.

Raknes, Ola (2004) *Wilhelm Reich and orgonomy,* Princeton: American College of Orgonomy Press

Rancière, Jacques (2004) *The politics of aesthetics,* London: Continuum.

Reich, Peter (2015) *A book of dreams,* London: John Blake Publishing.

Reich, Wilhelm (1945) *The sexual revolution: toward a self-governing character structure,* New York: Orgone institute press.

Reich, Wilhelm (1946) *The mass psychology of fascism,* New York: Orgone Institute Press.

Reich, Wilhelm (1949) *Ether, God and devil,* Rangeley: Orgone Institute Press

Reich, Wilhelm (1951) *Cosmic superimposition: Man's Orgonotic Roots in Nature,* Rangeley: Orgone Institute Press

Reich, Wilhelm (1967) *Reich speaks of Freud,* New York: Farrar, Straus and Giroux.

Reich, Wilhelm (1970) *The function of the orgasm,* New York: Farrar, Straus and Giroux.

Reich, Wilhelm (1971) *The murder of Christ*, New York: Farrar, Straus and Giroux.

Reich, Wilhelm (1973) *Selected writings: An introduction to orgonomy*, New York: Farrar, Straus and Giroux.

Reich, Wilhelm (1973b) *The cancer biopathy*, New York: Farrar, Straus and Giroux.

Reich, Wilhelm (1976) *People in trouble*, New York: Farrar, Straus and Giroux.

Reich, Wilhelm (1982) *The bioelectrical investigation of sexuality and anxiety*, New York: Farrar, Straus and Giroux.

Reich, Wilhelm (1994) *Beyond psychology: Letters and journals 1934-1939*, New York: Farrar, Straus and Giroux.

Ripple, William, and Robert Beschta (2004) "Wolves and the ecology of fear: can predation risk structure ecosystems?" *AIBS Bulletin*, 54.8 (2004): 755-766.

Rogers, Everett (1962) *Diffusion of innovations*, New York: Free Press of Glencoe.

Sartre, Jean-Paul (1966) *Being and nothingess*, New York: Washington Square Press.

Schmitt, Carl (1996) *The concept of the political*, Chicago: University of Chicago Press.

Siegworth, Gregory &, Melissa Gregg (2010) "An inventory of shimmers" in Gregg and Seigworth (eds) *The affect theory reader*, Durham: Duke University Press.

Sennett, Richard (2008) *The craftsman*, New Haven: Yale University Press.

Simmel, Georg (1957) "Fashion," *American Journal of Sociology* 62 (6): 541-558.

Sloterdijk, Peter (2010) *Rage and time: A psychopolitical investigation*, New York: Columbia University Press.

Steele, Valerie (1996) *Fetish: Fashion, sex and power*. New York: Oxford University Press.

Strick, James (2015) *Wilhelm Reich: Biologist*, Cambridge: Harvard University Press.

Theweleit, Klaus (1985) *Male fantasies, Vol. 1: Women, floods, bodies, history*, Minneapolis: University of Minnesota Press.

Tiger, Lionel & Robin Fox (1971) *The imperial animal*, New York: Holt, Rinehart & Winston.

Tonnesen, Morten (2012) "Semiogenesis," in Donald Favareau, Paul Cobley & Kalevi Kull (eds) (2012) *A more developed sign*, Tartu: Tartu University Press.

von Uexkull, Jacob (2010/1934) *A Foray into the worlds of animals and humans: with a theory of meaning*, Minneapolis: University of Minnesota Press.

Veblen, Thorstein (1899) *The theory of the leisure class*, New York: Macmillan.

Wark, McKenzie (2004) *A hacker manifesto*, Cambridge: Harvard University Press.

Weil, Simone (2005) "The Iliad, or the poem of force", in Simone Weil and Rachel Bespaloff (eds), *War and the Iliad*, New York: New York Review Books.

Weiss, Gail (1999) *Body images: Embodiment as intercorporeality*, London: Routledge.

Wenders, Wim (1989) *Notebook on cities and clothes*, documentary movie.

Wheeler, Wendy (2006) *The whole creature: Complexity, biosemiotics, and the evolution of culture*, London: Lawrence & Wishart.

Wilson, Edward (1975) *Sociobiology: The new synthesis*, Cambridge: Belknap.

Young, Iris (2005) *On female body experience*, Oxford: Oxford University Press.

ACKNOWLEDGMENTS

The author would like to thank the GIDEST fellows at The New School for valuable feedback on early drafts of a vitalist perspective on fashion and violence, Ari Elefterin for work on research contraptions and documentation, Daye Hwang for enriching an embodied approach to fashion and neuroscience, and Aaron Sechler for vital exchange of ideas.

For readers interested in Reich's legacy, I would recomment to visit and donate to the Wilhelm Reich Infant Trust (www.wilhelmreichtrust.org), and for an undistorted history of Reich's work please watch the documentary *Love, Work, Knowledge-The Life and Trials of Wilhelm Reich* (loveworkknowledge.com).

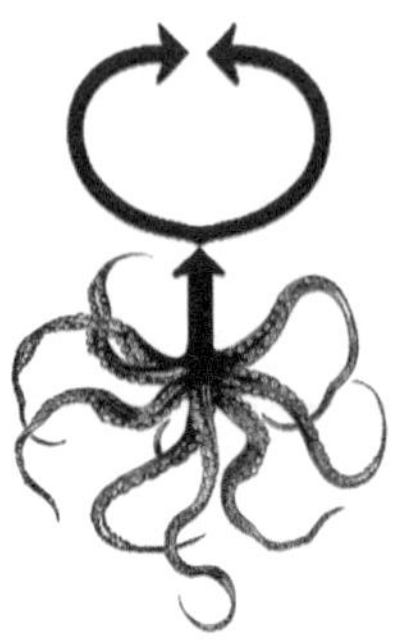

A last note on the transformation of Reich's symbol of functional identity/antithesis on the back cover of this volume (and above). Adding tentacles to this symbol has a "designerly" addition to Reich's original ideas. It serves to reveal a key insight brought from Reich into fashion. By adding limbs, pseudopodia, antennae, or tentacles to the core or source of the living energy, the new symbol highlights a crucial lesson from the biosocial approach to fashion. That fashion has *tentaculum*, from the Latin "to feel" and "to try." It reaches out, feeling, touching, while simultaneously entangling its prey. These appendages extends from the body itself. The source of fashion is life, and there is not only light at this core, but a seeming endless depth. Fashion has this uncanny and feral deepness: if we gaze long into it, the abyss will look back at us.